JAMESTOWN

Heritage

READERS

Book J

Lee Mountain, Ed.D.
University of Houston, Texas

Sharon Crawley, Ed.D.
Florida Atlantic University

Edward Fry, Ph.D.
Professor Emeritus
Rutgers University

Jamestown Publishers
Providence, Rhode Island

Favorite Children's Classics

ILLUSTRATED BY THE BEST ARTISTS
FROM THE PAST AND PRESENT

Jamestown Heritage Readers, Book F
Catalog No. 956
Catalog No. 956H, Hardcover Edition

© 1991 by Jamestown Publishers, Inc.

Cover and text design by Deborah Hulsey Christie
Cover and border illustrations by Pamela R. Levy

Printed in the United States of America

2 3 4 5 6 HA 97 96 95 94 93

ISBN 0-89061-956-5
ISBN 0-89061-715-5, Hardcover Edition

C·O·N·T·E·N·T·S

ONE
Tales Retold

1 Casey at the Bat 10
by ERNEST THAYER

2 How Ol' Paul Changed the Map of America 16
from YANKEE DOODLE'S COUSINS
by ANNE BURNETT MALCOLMSON

3 True Story 28
by SHEL SILVERSTEIN

4 Jill Is Given a Task by Aslan 30
from THE SILVER CHAIR
by C. S. LEWIS

5 A Word 42
by EMILY DICKINSON

6 ¿Qué es poesía?
(What Is Poetry?) 44
by GUSTAVO ADOLFO BÉCQUER

7 The Raven 46
by EDGAR ALLAN POE

8 The Scotty Who Knew Too Much 56
by JAMES THURBER

9   **The Little Girl and the Wolf**   59
by JAMES THURBER

10   **The Wolf in Sheep's Clothing**   60
from AESOP'S FABLES

11   **Matilda, Who Told Lies**   62
by HILAIRE BELLOC

12   **For the Love of a Man**   68
from THE CALL OF THE WILD
by JACK LONDON

13   **The Cremation of Sam McGee**   74
by ROBERT W. SERVICE

T W O

Here and There, Then and Now

1   **The Adventure of the Dancing Men**   84
by SIR ARTHUR CONAN DOYLE

2   **A Creed**   106
by EDWIN MARKHAM

3   **Psalm of Life**   108
from the poem
by HENRY WADSWORTH LONGFELLOW

4   **Before Olympic Medals**   110
from WILMA
by WILMA RUDOLPH

5   **The Runner**   118
by WALT WHITMAN

6   **Being Reasonable**   120
by BENJAMIN FRANKLIN

7   **Comments on a Proverb**   122
by BURR SHAFER

8   **Journal**   123
by RALPH WALDO EMERSON

9   **The Wind and the Sun**   124
from AESOP'S FABLES

10   **Pioneering by Lake Ontario**   126
from PICTURES OF CANADA
by CATHARINE TRAILL

11   **Stopping by Woods on a Snowy Evening**   136
by ROBERT FROST

12   **Give Me Liberty or Give Me Death**   138
by PATRICK HENRY

13   **These Are the Times That Try Men's Souls**   139
from THE AMERICAN CRISIS
by THOMAS PAINE

14   **Gettysburg Address**   140
by ABRAHAM LINCOLN

15   **Etched across the Pages of History**   144
from LETTER FROM A BIRMINGHAM JAIL
by MARTIN LUTHER KING, JR.

16   **Mother to Son**   146
by LANGSTON HUGHES

17   **My Little Son**   148
from the MAKAH

18   **A Runaway**   150
by SAIGYŌ HOSHI

19   **The Road Not Taken**   152
by ROBERT FROST

THREE
The Whole Chapter

Rikki-Tikki-Tavi   156
from THE JUNGLE BOOK
by RUDYARD KIPLING

FOUR
Nature and Nonsense

1   **The Blue Jay Yarn**   174
by MARK TWAIN

2   **The Sunflower**   183
a traditional Japanese poem

3   **Apollo and the Sunflower**   184
by THOMAS BULFINCH

4   **The Angler and the Fish**   186
from AESOP'S FABLES

5 **How Jahdu Became Himself** 188
from THE TIME-AGO TALES OF JAHDU
by VIRGINIA HAMILTON

6 **Gulliver in the Land of the Giants** 203
from GULLIVER'S TRAVELS
by JONATHAN SWIFT

7 **A Girl Like You** 211
translated from the Chinese by Isaac Victor Headland
from the book MEI LI
by THOMAS HANDFORTH

8 **The Story of Fidgety Philip** 212
by HEINRICH HOFFMANN

9 **"Run Faster!" Said the Queen** 214
from THROUGH THE LOOKING-GLASS
by LEWIS CARROLL

10 **Second Fig** 216
by EDNA ST. VINCENT MILLAY

11 **A Retrieved Reformation** 218
by O. HENRY

Acknowledgments 231

Illustration Credits 235

UNIT ONE

*Tales
Retold*

Casey at the Bat

by

ERNEST THAYER

The outlook wasn't brilliant for the Mudville nine that day.
The score was four to two with but one inning left to play.
And so when Cooley died at first and Barrows did the same,
A sickly silence fell upon the patrons of the game.

A straggling few got up to go in deep despair. The rest
Clung to that hope which springs eternal in the human breast.
They thought if only Casey could but get a whack at that—
We'd put up even money now, with Casey at the bat.

But Flynn preceded Casey, as did likewise Jimmy Blake.
The former was a no-good, and the latter was a fake.
So, on that stricken multitude, grim melancholy sat
For there seemed but little chance of Casey's getting to the bat.

But Flynn let drive a single to the wonderment of all.
And Blake, the much despised, tore the cover off the ball.
And when the dust had lifted, and they saw what had occurred,
There was Jimmy safe at second, and Flynn a-hugging third.

Then from five thousand throats or more went up a lusty yell.
It rumbled through the valley. It rattled in the dell.
It knocked upon the mountainside and echoed in the flat
For Casey, mighty Casey, was advancing to the bat.

There was ease in Casey's manner as he stepped into his place.
There was pride in Casey's bearing and a smile on Casey's face.
And when responding to the cheers, he lightly doffed his hat,
No stranger in the crowd could doubt 'twas Casey at the bat.

Ten thousand eyes were on him as he rubbed his hands in dirt.
Five thousand tongues applauded as he wiped them on his shirt.
Then while the writhing pitcher ground the ball into his hip,
Defiance gleamed in Casey's eye, a sneer curled Casey's lip.

And now the leather-covered sphere came hurtling through the air,
And Casey stood a-watching it in lofty grandeur there.
Close by the sturdy batsman, the ball unheeded sped—
"That ain't my style," said Casey. "Strike one!" the umpire said.

From the benches black with people, there went up a muffled roar,
Like the beating of the storm waves on a stern and distant shore.
"Kill him! Kill the umpire!" shouted someone in the stand.
And it's likely they'd have killed him had not Casey raised his hand.

With a smile of Christian charity great Casey's visage shone.
He stilled the rising tumult. He bade the game go on.
He signaled to the pitcher, and once more the spheroid flew.
But Casey still ignored it, and the umpire cried, "Strike two!"

"Fraud!" cried the maddened thousands, and an echo answered, "Fraud!"
But one scornful look from Casey and the multitude was awed.
They saw his face grow stern and cold. They saw his muscles strain.
And they knew that Casey would not let that ball go by again.

The sneer is gone from Casey's lips. His teeth are clenched in hate.
He pounds with hideous violence his bat upon the plate.
And now the pitcher holds the ball, and now he lets it go.
And now the air is shattered by the force of Casey's blow.

Oh, somewhere in this favored land the sun is shining bright.
Somewhere bands are playing. And somewhere hearts are light.
And somewhere men are laughing. And somewhere children shout.
But there is no joy in Mudville—mighty Casey has struck out.

How Ol' Paul Changed the Map of America

from

YANKEE DOODLE'S COUSINS

by

ANNE BURNETT MALCOLMSON

The map of Real America must have been very dull in the days before Paul Bunyan changed it. No mountains, no lakes, no rivers! Nothing but plain, flat land! You could roller skate from the Atlantic to the Pacific, if you wanted to do such a thing.

Whether or not Paul intended to make any changes, we don't know. Wherever he went, however, strange and wonderful things took place.

He had a remarkable effect on the weather. When Paul was around, the weatherman lost his head and the seasons turned somersaults. There was the Hot Hot Hot Summer, for instance. It happened soon after Hot Biscuit Slim came to Onion River.

Slim told Paul about the joys of eating corn-on-the-cob. He described it so well that Paul could feel the hot butter trickling down his chin. His mouth watered. He had to taste some. So he planted the whole state of Iowa with sweet corn and licked his chops.

17

Paul never had his corn-on-the-cob, however. The weather turned hot, hotter, hottest. The corn shot up out of the ground like smoke from a fire. The kernels burst from their ears and fell to the ground. Under the blazing sun, they popped as they fell. Soon Iowa was covered four feet deep with popcorn.

That wasn't the end of it, either. A big wind blew in from the northeast and carried the corn to Kansas. There it fell from the skies like a blizzard. Thousands of cattle, grazing on the Kansas fields, thought it was snow and promptly froze to death.

Then there was the spring the Rains Came Up From China. Paul and his boys were logging off the country around the Cascade Mountains in Oregon. They had only started the job when it began to rain. It didn't rain down from the skies. It rained up from the earth. For days on end, the ground oozed rain. Some drained off and formed the Cascade River with its lovely waterfalls. In other places it never stopped. It's still bubbling up in the hot springs and little geysers of Yosemite Park. Incidentally, it was from this season that Mount Rainier took its name.

Some years later, after Paul had returned to his Onion River Camp, he became restless. He'd heard about the cypress forests of Louisiana, and he wanted to see them. But before he reached them, it began to rain again. This time the rain fell down, all night, but it was all of a bright red color. For sixteen days and seventeen nights the Red Rain fell. Some of it is still running off in the Red River of Arkansas.

On this walk to Louisiana Paul got sand in his shoes. Of course, sand isn't comfortable to walk on. So he sat down on the Ozarks and poured out the sand into a ragged pile. This pile is known as the Kiamichi Mountains of Eastern Oklahoma.

I could go on all night telling you about Paul's special weather. There was the Year of the Hard Winter. The words froze in the air as soon as they were spoken. Several of the lumberjacks bumped into them in the dark and cut their foreheads. In the spring, when the conversations thawed out all at once, the noise was terrible.

Paul's most important work in changing the map, however, was done without any help from the weatherman. Just as in the case of the Kiamichi, he did it alone, sometimes by accident. Even Babe did some of it.

If you've ever been to North Dakota you know that there are huge tracks in the rocks. Scientists say that these are the tracks of dinosaurs. Dinosaurs were huge animals that lived in North America long before man became man. Of course, we know that they are Babe's hoof-prints.

There are many iron mines in Northern Michigan near Lake Superior. It was Paul who opened them in order to find metal for Babe's shoes. He opened a new one every time the ox needed to be shod.

And then there is the story about one of Paul's smaller feats. This took place when he fought the Big Swede on top of the Mountain That Stood on Its Head. After the battle, when the dust had cleared away, nothing

19

remained of the strange mountain but a pile of broken earth. This is what we call the Bad Lands of the Dakotas.

Geography isn't a matter of maps alone. It takes in other things, such as businesses and farm products. Paul dabbled even in these. He went hunting in Canada one fine autumn morning. His little hunting dog Elmer suddenly found the track of a huge buck. Together Paul and Elmer trailed the buck down the St. Lawrence Valley, across Ontario. In Michigan Paul managed to shoot—but his shot merely wounded the animal. On and on raced the buck, the hunter after him. He plunged into the icy waters of Lake Michigan and struggled across. But the effort of swimming and the loss of blood were too much. The big buck fell dead on the opposite shore, right on the Chicago waterfront.

Paul didn't want the meat. He had a large dinner waiting for him back in Onion River. So he sold the carcass to a butcher, who cut it up and used it to start the meat-packing business, for which Chicago is famous.

The map of North America owes a great deal to a sad year in Paul's life. Babe became ill. His bright blue coat faded and grew dull. His lovely big eyes rolled unhappily. Paul and Johnny Inkslinger got down all their books on medicine and tried to cure him. Nothing did any good. At last Johnny suggested that a change in climate would help. Paul was only too glad to do anything that might cure his adored pet. Within an hour he had the bunkhouses packed and was off on his long trip west.

This time, of course, the procession moved slowly. Paul carried the bunkhouses on his shoulders and

Brimstone Bill walked beside Babe, feeding him medicine and keeping cold packs on his head. It was a tiresome trip. In Colorado they stopped to rest. The Big Swede, in order to mark the trail, set up a pile of rocks. Paul helped him and stuck in a pike, or pole, in order to top it off. This has since become known as Pike's Peak.

From Colorado the party moved northwest. Paul had heard about the wonderful sulphur springs which cure all illnesses. In one corner of Wyoming he thought he heard one of these springs bubbling under ground. Here he stopped and started to dig a drinking hole for Babe. He'd gotten down about a hundred feet without striking water, when the hole dropped out from under. This surprised him so that he dropped his spade. Down, down, down it fell until it was completely lost from sight in the middle of the earth.

Paul was about to dig another hole with another spade, when he heard a rumbling and a hissing below. Whish! Like a shot out of a gun, his spade flew into the air. It was completely melted. It was carried up on a column of steam. High in the air it hung for a moment and then sank back into the hole.

Ever since that day, every hour on the hour, the spade has been shot up into the air and then has fallen back into the hole. Some years ago the Government named it Old Faithful and put Yellowstone Park around it.

The long trip over the Rockies was hard on the sick ox. By the time they reached Utah, he was unable to go any farther. His fever was high. He put out his pale tongue and feebly licked Paul's hand. His eyes looked up

21

miserably as much as to say "Good-bye." Paul and Johnny were sure he was going to die.

The big lumberjack sadly dug a grave for his beloved Babe. As he dug he wept bitter salt tears. At last he was crying so hard he had to stop digging. He sat down

beside the grave and let himself go. The tears gushed from his eyes.

Someone touched him on the shoulder. It was Brimstone Bill. Paul, of course, thought that Bill had come to tell him that Babe was dead. He wept more than ever. Not until a soft warm tongue licked his cheek did he realize that Babe was better. By some miracle the ox had lived through the crisis. He was still weak, but he was going to get well.

Paul jumped up in joy. He hugged Babe and patted him and acted like a crazy man. He set off immediately for the pleasant climate of California, so that Babe could take it easy as he was growing stronger. But the grave full of salt tears was left behind. Great Salt Lake is there today, a monument to Paul's sorrow.

After a winter in California, Babe grew well and strong. Word came to Paul about the Stonewood Forests in Arizona. They were not far away, so he and Babe walked over one evening to see. The trees were as hard as rock. The wood was colored in lovely reds and yellows and browns. Altogether Paul thought it the most interesting logging country he had ever seen. He planned to bring his camp over and to start cutting right away.

Unfortunately, Babe's illness had left him with a bad case of hay fever. The dry, stone dust of the forest floor got up his nose. He sneezed. He sneezed again and again. His eyes began to run. Paul saw at once that this was no country for an animal with hay fever. So he gave up his plans and hurried back to California. Babe's sneezes had another effect, though. They raised the dust

23

storms which blow across Oklahoma and Texas, burying farms and ranches under their white powder.

On the way back to California, Paul discovered a little river, shaded by walls of rock. The hot sandy floor of Arizona had burned his feet. The water looked cool and inviting. Paul pulled off his shoes and waded for a while. As he waded he let his pickaxe drag in the water behind him. To this day you can see the track it made. We call it the Grand Canyon of the Colorado River.

Paul Bunyan hated to hire himself out to another boss. He wanted to be the boss himself. Once, at least, he did agree to work for another man. The government needed a new bay, or sound. The President sent surveyors out to the West to find a good place. They suggested the coast of Washington. This sounded good to the President and he hired the Dan Puget Construction Company to do the work. Puget was a good man. But he was a little man, not used to doing things on Paul's scale. He worked and worked and worked. Alas, the job was too big for him.

He sent for Paul and begged him to come and help. Bunyan didn't like the idea of working for a man who couldn't do his own work properly. But he was kind-hearted. He felt sorry for Mr. Puget and agreed to his terms.

After one brief look around the country, Paul knew exactly what to do. Steam-shovels and pile-drivers were mere toys to him. He needed a glacier. He drove Babe up to Alaska, hitched him to a glacier with the sharp side down, and started back to the States.

They had hardly left Alaska before they had an

accident. A schoolteacher with a pink parasol crossed the road. Most bulls go mad at the sight of the color red. Babe went mad when he saw pink. To make matters worse, the schoolmarm stopped in her tracks when she saw the enormous ox and his driver. In her surprise she twirled her parasol around and around, right under Babe's nose.

The big blue ox couldn't help it. He lowered his head, and pawed the ground angrily. Fire and smoke poured out from his nostrils. With a bellow of pain he rushed at the pink object and snatched it from her hand. Then

25

off he went like a tornado. He roared up and down the coast of British Columbia and the coast of Washington. The glacier dragged behind him like a driverless plow. It was several hours before they could calm him down. When at last they led him off to the stable, there lay a great gash in the earth. Puget Sound was dug. Not only Puget Sound, but the Hood Canal as well!

The biggest change Paul made in the map of North America was one of the first of all. It took place while he was building the Onion River Camp. He needed reservoirs for drinking water, both for his men and for the animals about the place. Babe, of course, drank a whole lake full every morning before breakfast. So the lumberjack dug the Great Lakes. He started with Lake Ontario. This proved to be too small to be practical. He moved a little farther west and dug Lake Erie, several sizes larger. These two little lakes did very well until his camp began to grow. When the Big Swede and Johnny Inkslinger joined his company he needed still larger reservoirs.

He dug Huron and Michigan, in the hope that they would prove to be enough. Not until he had finished the largest lake of all, Superior, did he have a really good water supply.

Babe and Brimstone Bill filled the lakes. They hauled water from the Atlantic Ocean on big sleds. Once Babe tripped over a small hill in the Huron Range. The sled turned over and spilled the big tank of water. Down to the south it poured in a rushing flood. Paul realized that the whole country would be flooded. Fields and towns and railroads would all be carried down to the Gulf of Mexico. To avoid disaster he grabbed up his spade. He ran ahead of the water, digging a channel for it to flow into. On either side of the ditch great spadefuls of earth were tossed into the air. They landed in long even piles, one to the east, one to the west. Paul Bunyan reached the Gulf just in time. The water spilled safely out into the ocean stream without doing any damage.

The ditch, as you may have guessed, is still filled with a great river, the Mississippi. The ridges of earth thrown up by Paul's spade are none other than the Rocky Mountains and the Appalachians. Wouldn't the map of North America be dull without these?

True Story

by

SHEL SILVERSTEIN

This morning I jumped on my horse
And went out for a ride,
And some wild outlaws chased me
And they shot me in the side.
So I crawled into a wildcat's cave
To find a place to hide,
But some pirates found me sleeping there,
And soon they had me tied
To a pole and built a fire
Under me—I almost cried
Till a mermaid came and cut me loose
And begged to be my bride,
So I said I'd come back Wednesday
But I must admit I lied.
Then I ran into a jungle swamp
But I forgot my guide
And I stepped into some quicksand,
And no matter how I tried
I couldn't get out, until I met
A water snake named Clyde,
Who pulled me to some cannibals
Who planned to have me fried.
But an eagle came and swooped me up
And through the air we flied,
But he dropped me in a boiling lake
A thousand miles wide.
And you'll never guess what I did then—
I DIED.

Jill Is Given a Task by Aslan

from

THE SILVER CHAIR

by

C. S. LEWIS

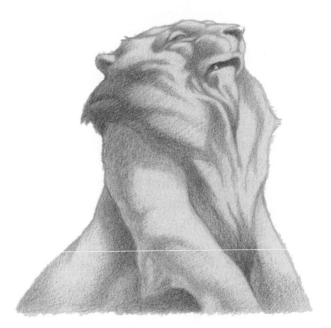

In *The Silver Chair* and in the other books in the Narnia series, boys and girls from this world find their way into another world, a world ruled by the noble lion Aslan. In these pages from *The Silver Chair,* you will meet a girl named Jill Pole and a boy named Eustace Scrubb. Eustace has been to Narnia before, has told Jill about it, and has wondered about getting there again.

As this part of the story opens, they are being pursued by the bullies of their school, a group called "Them." Jill and Eustace hope to escape through a door in the stone wall around the school grounds, but they are afraid it will be locked.

ustace and Jill, now both very hot and very grubby from going along bent almost double under the laurels, panted up to the wall. And there was the door, shut as usual.

"It's sure to be no good," said Eustace with his hand on the handle; and then, "O-o-oh. By Gum!!" For the handle turned and the door opened.

A moment before, both of them had meant to get through that doorway in double quick time, if by any chance the door was not locked. But when the door actually opened, they both stood stock still. For what they saw was quite different from what they had expected.

They had expected to see the grey, heathery slope of the moor going up and up to join the dull autumn sky. Instead, a blaze of sunshine met them. It poured through the doorway as the light of a June day pours into a garage when you open the door. It made the drops of water on the grass glitter like beads and showed up the dirtiness of Jill's tear-stained face. And the sunlight was coming from what certainly did look like a different world—what they could see of it. They saw smooth turf, smoother and brighter than Jill had ever seen before, and blue sky, and, darting to and fro, things so bright that they might have been jewels or huge butterflies.

Although she had been longing for something like this, Jill felt frightened. She looked at Scrubb's face and saw that he was frightened too.

31

"Come on, Pole," he said in a breathless voice.

"Can we get back? Is it safe?" asked Jill.

At that moment a voice shouted from behind, a mean, spiteful little voice. "Now then, Pole," it squeaked. "Everyone knows you're there. Down you come." It was the voice of Edith Jackle, not one of Them herself but one of their hangers-on and tale-bearers.

"Quick!" said Scrubb. "Here. Hold hands. We mustn't get separated." And before she quite knew what was happening, he had grabbed her hand and pulled her through the door, out of the school grounds, out of England, out of our whole world into That Place.

The sound of Edith Jackle's voice stopped as suddenly as the voice on the radio when it is switched off. Instantly there was a quite different sound all about them. It came from those bright things overhead, which now turned out to be birds. They were making a riotous noise, but it was much more like music—rather advanced music which you don't quite take in at the first hearing—than birds' songs ever are in our world. Yet, in spite of the singing, there was a sort of background of immense silence. That silence, combined with the freshness of the air, made Jill think they must be on the top of a very high mountain.

Scrubb still had her by the hand and they were walking forward, staring about them on every side. Jill saw that huge trees, rather like cedars but bigger, grew in every direction. But as they did not grow close together, and as there was not undergrowth, this did not prevent one from seeing a long way into the forest to

left and right. And as far as Jill's eye could reach, it was
all the same—level turf, darting birds with yellow, or
dragonfly blue, or rainbow plumage, blue shadows, and
emptiness. There was not a breath of wind in that cool,
bright air. It was a very lonely forest.

Right ahead there were no trees; only blue sky. They
went straight on without speaking till suddenly Jill heard
Scrubb say, "Look out!" and felt herself jerked back. They
were at the very edge of a cliff.

Jill was one of those lucky people who have a good head for heights. She didn't mind in the least standing on the edge of a precipice. She was rather annoyed with Scrubb for pulling her back—"just as if I was a kid," she said—and she wrenched her hand out of his. When she saw how very white he had turned, she despised him.

"What's the matter?" she said. And to show that she was not afraid, she stood very near the edge indeed; in fact, a good deal nearer than even she liked. Then she looked down.

She now realized that Scrubb had some excuse for looking white, for no cliff in our world is to be compared with this. Imagine yourself at the top of the very highest cliff you know. And imagine yourself looking down to the very bottom. And then imagine that the precipice goes on below that, as far again, ten times as far, twenty times as far. And when you've looked down all that distance imagine little white things that might, at first glance, be mistaken for sheep, but presently you realize that they are clouds—not little wreathes of mist but the enormous white, puffy clouds which are themselves as big as most mountains. And at last, in between those clouds, you get your first glimpse of the real bottom, so far away that you can't make out whether it's field or wood, or land or water: further below those clouds than you are above them.

Jill stared at it. Then she thought that perhaps, after all, she would step back a foot or so from the edge; but she didn't like to for fear of what Scrubb would think. Then she suddenly decided that she didn't care what he thought, and that she would jolly well get away from the horrible edge and never laugh at anyone for not liking heights again. But when she tried to move, she found she couldn't. Her legs seemed to have turned into putty. Everything was swimming before her eyes.

"What are you doing, Pole? Come back—blithering little idiot!" shouted Scrubb. But his voice seemed to be coming from a long way off. She felt him grabbing at her. But by now she had no control over her own arms and legs. There was a moment's struggling on the cliff edge. Jill was too frightened and dizzy to know quite what she was doing, but two things she remembered as long as she lived (they often came back to her in dreams). One was that she had wrenched herself free of Scrubb's clutches; the other was that, at the same moment, Scrubb himself, with a terrified scream, had lost his balance and gone hurtling to the depths.

Fortunately she was given no time to think over what she had done. Some huge, brightly colored animal had rushed to the edge of the cliff. It was lying down, leaning over, and (this was the odd thing) blowing. Not roaring or snorting but just blowing from its wide-opened mouth; blowing out as steadily as a vacuum cleaner sucks in. Jill was lying so close to the creature that she could feel the breath vibrating steadily through its body. She was lying still because she couldn't get up. She was nearly fainting: indeed, she wished she could really faint, but faints don't come for the asking. At last she saw, far away below her, a tiny black speck floating away from the cliff and slightly upwards. As it rose, it

35

also got further away. By the time it was nearly on a level with the cliff top it was so far off that she lost sight of it. It was obviously moving away from them at a great speed. Jill couldn't help thinking that the creature at her side was blowing it away.

So she turned and looked at the creature. It was a lion.

Without a glance at Jill the Lion rose to its feet and gave one last blow. Then, as if satisfied with its work, it turned and stalked slowly away, back into the forest.

"It must be a dream, it must, it must," said Jill to herself. "I'll wake up in a moment." But it wasn't, and she didn't. "I do wish we'd never come to this dreadful place," said Jill. "I don't believe Scrubb knew any more about it than I do. Or if he did, he had no business to bring me here without warning me what it was like. It's not my fault he fell over that cliff. If he'd left me alone we should both be all right." Then she remembered again the scream that Scrubb had given when he fell, and burst into tears.

Crying is all right in its way while it lasts. But you have to stop sooner or later and then you still have to decide what to do. When Jill stopped, she found she was dreadfully thirsty. She had been lying face downward, and now she sat up. The birds had ceased singing and there was perfect silence except for one small persistent sound which seemed to come a good distance away. She listened carefully and felt almost sure it was the sound of running water.

Jill got up and looked round her very carefully. There

was no sign of the Lion; but there were so many trees
about that it might easily be quite close without her
seeing it. For all she knew, there might be several lions.
But her thirst was very bad now, and she plucked up her
courage to go and look for that running water. She went
on tiptoes, stealing cautiously from tree to tree, and
stopping to peer round her at every step.

The wood was so still that it was not difficult to decide
where the sound was coming from. It grew clearer every
moment and, sooner than she expected, she came to an
open glade and saw the stream, bright as glass, running
across the turf a stone's throw away from her. But although the sight of the water made her feel ten times
thirstier than before, she didn't rush forward and drink.
She stood as still as if she had been turned into stone,
with her mouth wide open. And she had a very good
reason; just on this side of the stream lay the Lion.

It lay with its head raised and its two fore-paws out in

front of it, like the lions in Trafalgar Square. She knew at once that it had seen her, for its eyes looked straight into hers for a moment and then turned away—as if it knew her quite well and didn't think much of her.

"If I run away, it'll be after me in a moment," thought Jill. "And if I go on, I shall run straight into its mouth." Anyway, she couldn't have moved if she had tried, and she couldn't take her eyes off it. How long this lasted, she could not be sure; it seemed like hours. And the thirst became so bad that she almost felt she would not mind being eaten by the Lion if only she could be sure of getting a mouthful of water first.

"If you're thirsty, you may drink."

They were the first words she had heard since Scrubb had spoken to her on the edge of the cliff. For a second she stared here and there, wondering who had spoken. Then the voice said again, "If you are thirsty, come and drink," and of course she remembered what Scrubb had said about animals talking in that other world, and realized that it was the Lion speaking. Anyway, she had seen its lips move this time, and the voice was not like a man's. It was deeper, wilder, and stronger; a sort of heavy, golden voice. It did not make her any less frightened than she had been before, but it made her frightened in rather a different way.

"Are you not thirsty?" said the Lion.

"I'm *dying* of thirst," said Jill.

"Then drink," said the Lion.

"May I—could I—would you mind going away while I do?" said Jill.

The Lion answered this only by a look and a very low growl. And as Jill gazed at its motionless bulk, she realized that she might as well have asked the whole mountain to move aside for her convenience.

The delicious rippling noise of the stream was driving her nearly frantic.

"Will you promise not to—do anything to me, if I do come?" said Jill.

"I make no promise," said the Lion.

Jill was so thirsty now that, without noticing it, she had come a step nearer.

"*Do* you eat girls?" she said.

"I have swallowed up girls and boys, women and men, kings and emperors, cities and realms," said the Lion. It didn't say this as if it were boasting, nor as if it were sorry, nor as if it were angry. It just said it.

"I daren't come and drink," said Jill.

"Then you will die of thirst," said the Lion.

"Oh dear!" said Jill, coming another step nearer. "I suppose I must go and look for another stream then."

"There is no other stream," said the Lion.

It never occurred to Jill to disbelieve the Lion—no one who had seen his stern face could do that—and her mind suddenly made itself up. It was the worst thing she had ever had to do but she went forward to the stream, knelt down, and began scooping up water in her hand. It was the coldest, most refreshing water she had ever tasted. You didn't need to drink much of it, for it quenched your thirst at once. Before she tasted it she had been intending to make a dash away from the Lion the moment she had finished. Now, she realized that this would be on the whole the most dangerous thing of all. She got up and stood there with her lips still wet from drinking.

"Come here," said the Lion. And she had to. She was almost between its front paws now, looking straight into its face. But she couldn't stand that for long; she dropped her eyes.

"Human Child," said the Lion, "Where is the Boy?"

"He fell over the cliff," said Jill, and added, "Sir." She didn't know what else to call him, and it sounded cheek to call him nothing.

"How did he come to do that, Human Child?"

"He was trying to stop me from falling, Sir."

"Why were you so near the edge, Human Child?"

"I was showing off, Sir."

"That is a very good answer, Human Child. Do so no more. And now" (here for the first time the Lion's face became a little less stern) "the Boy is safe. I have blown him to Narnia. But your task will be the harder because of what you have done."

"Please, what task, Sir?" said Jill.

"The task for which I called you and him here out of your own world."

This puzzled Jill very much. "It's mistaking me for someone else," she thought. She didn't dare to tell the Lion this, though she felt things would get into a dreadful muddle unless she did.

"Speak your thought, Human Child," said the Lion.

"I was wondering—I mean—could there be some mistake? Because nobody called me and Scrubb, you know. It was we who asked to come here. Scrubb said we were to call to—to Somebody—it was a name I wouldn't know—and perhaps the Somebody would let us in. And we did, and then we found the door open."

"You would not have called to me unless I had been calling to you," said the Lion.

"Then you are Somebody, Sir?" said Jill.

"I am. And now hear your task. Far from here in the land of Narnia there lives an aged King who is sad because he has no prince of his blood to be king after him. He has no heir because his only son was stolen from him many years ago and no one in Narnia knows where that Prince went or whether he is still alive. But he is. I lay on you this command, that you seek this lost Prince until either you have found him and brought him to his father's house, or else died in the attempt, or else gone back into your own world."

A Word

by

EMILY DICKINSON

A word is dead
When it is said,
  Some say.

I say it just
Begins to live
  That day.

¿Qué es poesía?

de

GUSTAVO ADOLFO BÉCQUER

¿Qué es poesía? dices mientras clavas
en mi pupila tu pupila azul;
¿Qué es poesía? ¿Y tú me lo preguntas?
Poesía . . . eres tú.

What Is Poetry?

by

GUSTAVO ADOLFO BÉCQUER

"**W**hat is poetry?" you say as you fix
Upon my eyes your eyes of blue.
What is poetry? And you ask me that?
Poetry . . . is you!

The Raven

by

EDGAR ALLAN POE

Once upon a midnight dreary, while I pondered, weak and weary,
Over many a quaint and curious volume of forgotten lore—
While I nodded, nearly napping, suddenly there came a tapping,
As of someone gently rapping, rapping at my chamber door.
" 'Tis some visitor," I muttered, "tapping at my chamber door—
      Only this and nothing more."

Ah, distinctly I remember it was in the bleak December;
And each separate dying ember wrought its ghost upon the floor.
Eagerly I wished the morrow;—vainly I had sought to borrow
From my books surcease of sorrow—sorrow for the lost Lenore—
For the rare and radiant maiden whom the angels name Lenore—
      Nameless *here* for evermore.

And the silken, sad, uncertain rustling of each purple curtain
Thrilled me—filled me with fantastic terrors never felt before;
So that now, to still the beating of my heart, I stood repeating
" 'Tis some visitor entreating entrance at my chamber door—
Some late visitor entreating entrance at my chamber door;—
      This it is and nothing more."

Presently my soul grew stronger; hesitating then no longer,
"Sir," said I, "or Madam, truly your forgiveness I implore;
But the fact is I was napping, and so gently you came rapping,
And so faintly you came tapping, tapping at my chamber door,
That I scarce was sure I heard you"—here I opened wide the door;—
      Darkness there and nothing more.

Deep into that darkness peering, long I stood there wondering, fearing,
Doubting, dreaming dreams no mortal ever dared to dream before;
But the silence was unbroken, and the stillness gave no token,
And the only word there spoken was the whispered word, "Lenore?"
This I whispered, and an echo murmured back the word, "Lenore!"
      Merely this and nothing more.

Back into the chamber turning, all my soul within me burning,
Soon again I heard a tapping somewhat louder than before.
"Surely," said I, "surely that is something at my window lattice;
Let me see, then, what thereat is, and this mystery explore—
Let my heart be still a moment and this mystery explore;—
      'Tis the wind and nothing more!"

Open here I flung the shutter, when, with many a flirt and flutter,
In there stepped a stately Raven of the saintly days of yore;
Not the least obeisance made he; not a minute stopped or stayed he;
But with mien of lord or lady, perched above my chamber door—
Perched upon a bust of Pallas just above my chamber door—
    Perched, and sat, and nothing more.

Then this ebony bird beguiling my sad fancy into smiling,
By the grave and stern decorum of the countenance it wore,
"Though thy crest be shorn and shaven, thou," I said, "art sure no craven,
Ghastly grim and ancient Raven wandering from the Nightly shore—
Tell me what thy lordly name is on the Night's Plutonian shore!"
    Quoth the Raven "Nevermore."

Much I marveled this ungainly fowl to hear discourse so plainly,
Though its answer little meaning—little relevancy bore;
For we cannot help agreeing that no living human being
Ever yet was blessed with seeing bird above his chamber door—
Bird or beast upon the sculptured bust above his chamber door,
    With such name as "Nevermore."

But the Raven, sitting lonely on the placid bust, spoke only
That one word, as if his soul in that one word he did outpour.
Nothing farther then he uttered—not a feather then he fluttered—
Till I scarcely more than muttered, "Other friends have flown before—
On the morrow *he* will leave me, as my Hopes have flown before."
      Then the bird said "Nevermore."

Startled at the stillness broken by reply so aptly spoken,
"Doubtless," said I, "what it utters is its only stock and store
Caught from some unhappy master whom unmerciful Disaster
Followed fast and followed faster till his songs one burden bore—
Till the dirges of his Hope that melancholy burden bore
      Of 'Never—nevermore.' "

But the Raven still beguiling my sad fancy into smiling,
Straight I wheeled a cushioned seat in front of bird, and bust and door;
Then, upon the velvet sinking, I betook myself to linking
Fancy unto fancy, thinking what this ominous bird of yore—
What this grim, ungainly, ghastly, gaunt and ominous bird of yore
      Meant in croaking "Nevermore."

This I sat engaged in guessing, but no syllable expressing
To the fowl whose fiery eyes now burned into my bosom's core;
This and more I sat divining, with my head at ease reclining
On the cushion's velvet lining that the lamp-light gloated o'er,
But whose velvet-violet lining with the lamp-light gloating o'er,
　　　She shall press, ah, nevermore!

Then, methought, the air grew denser, perfumed from an unseen censer
Swung by seraphim whose foot-falls tinkled on the tufted floor.
"Wretch!" I cried, "thy God hath lent thee—by these angels he hath sent thee
Respite—respite and nepenthe from the memories of Lenore;
Quaff, oh quaff this kind nepenthe and forget this lost Lenore!"
　　　Quoth the Raven "Nevermore."

"Prophet!" said I, "thing of evil!—prophet still, if bird or devil!
Whether Tempter sent, or whether tempest tossed thee here ashore,
Desolate yet all undaunted, on this desert land enchanted—
On this home by Horror haunted—tell me truly, I implore—
Is there—*is* there balm in Gilead?—tell me—tell me, I implore!"
　　　Quoth the Raven "Nevermore."

"Prophet!" said I, "thing of evil!—prophet still, if bird or devil!
By that Heaven that bends above us—by that God we both adore—
Tell this soul with sorrow laden if, within the distant Aidenn,
It shall clasp a sainted maiden whom the angels name Lenore—
Clasp a rare and radiant maiden whom the angels name Lenore."
       Quoth the Raven "Nevermore."

"Be that word our sign of parting, bird or fiend!" I shrieked, upstarting—
"Get thee back into the tempest and the Night's Plutonian shore!
Leave no black plume as a token of that lie thy soul hath spoken!
Leave my loneliness unbroken!—quit the bust above my door!
Take thy beak from out my heart, and take thy form from off my door!"
       Quoth the Raven "Nevermore."

And the Raven, never flitting, still is sitting, *still* is sitting
On the pallid bust of Pallas just above my chamber door;
And his eyes have all the seeming of a demon's that is dreaming,
And the lamp-light o'er him streaming throws his shadow on the floor;
And my soul from out that shadow that lies floating on the floor
       Shall be lifted—nevermore!

The Scotty Who Knew Too Much

by

JAMES THURBER

everal summers ago there was a Scotty who went to the country for a visit. He decided that all the farm dogs were cowards because they were afraid of a certain animal that had a white stripe down its back.

"You are a pussy-cat and I can lick you," the Scotty said to the farm dog who lived in the house where the Scotty was visiting. "I can lick the little animal with the white stripe, too. Show him to me."

"Don't you want to ask any questions about him?" said the farm dog.

"Naw," said the Scotty. "*You* ask the questions."

So the farm dog took the Scotty into the woods and showed him the white-striped animal, and the Scotty closed in on him, growling and slashing.

It was all over in a moment and the Scotty lay on his back.

When he came to, the farm dog said, "What happened?"

"He threw vitriol," said the Scotty, "but he never laid a glove on me."

A few days later the farm dog told the Scotty there was another animal all the farm dogs were afraid of.

"Lead me to him," said the Scotty. "I can lick anything that doesn't wear horseshoes."

"Don't you want to ask any questions about him?" said the farm dog.

"Naw," said the Scotty. "Just show me where he hangs out."

So the farm dog led him to a place in the woods and pointed out the little animal when he came along.

"A clown," said the Scotty, "a pushover." And he closed in, leading with his left and exhibiting some mighty fancy footwork.

In less than a second the Scotty was flat on his back, and when he woke up, the farm dog was pulling quills out of him.

"What happened?" said the farm dog.

"He pulled a knife on me," said the Scotty, "but at least I've learned how you fight out here in the country, and now I am going to beat you up."

So he closed in on the farm dog, holding his nose with one front paw to ward off the vitriol and covering his eyes with the other front paw to keep out the knives.

The Scotty couldn't see his opponent and he couldn't smell his opponent and he was so badly beaten that he had to be taken back to the city and put in a nursing home.

Moral: It is better to ask some of the questions than to know all the answers.

The Little Girl and the Wolf

by JAMES THURBER

One afternoon a big wolf waited in a dark forest for a little girl to come along carrying a basket of food to her grandmother. Finally a little girl did come along and she was carrying a basket of food. "Are you carrying that basket to your grandmother?" asked the wolf. The little girl said yes, she was. So the wolf asked her where her grandmother lived and the little girl told him and he disappeared into the wood.

When the little girl opened the door of her grandmother's house she saw that there was somebody in bed with a nightcap and nightgown on. She had approached no nearer than twenty-five feet from the bed when she saw that it was not her grandmother but the wolf, for even in a nightcap a wolf does not look any more like your grandmother than the Metro-Goldwyn lion looks like Calvin Coolidge. So the little girl took an automatic out of her basket and shot the wolf dead.

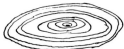

Moral: It is not so easy to fool little girls
nowadays as it used to be.

59

The Wolf in Sheep's Clothing

from

AESOP'S FABLES

A wolf once found the skin of a sheep on the ground. It was woolly and white and warm.

"If I put this on, I would look just like a sheep," said the wolf. "Then I could slip into the sheepfold. No one would notice me, so it would be easy to carry off a lamb for my dinner."

The wolf put the big woolly sheepskin over his back and his head, and it covered him well. With no trouble at all, he slipped among the sheep when they were out in the pasture.

Before the wolf could grab a lamb, the shepherd came out. He looked over all his sheep, intending to choose a big one to kill and cook for his dinner.

Only after the shepherd had killed the biggest one in the fold did he notice his mistake.

"Ah, well," said he. "It is a fitting end for a wolf in a sheep's clothing."

Don't pretend to be something you are not.

Matilda, Who Told Lies

by

HILAIRE BELLOC

Matilda told such dreadful lies,

It made one gasp and stretch one's eyes;
Her Aunt, who, from her earliest youth,
Had kept a strict regard for truth,

Attempted to believe Matilda:
The effort very nearly killed her,
And would have done so, had not she
Discovered this infirmity.
For once, towards the close of day,
Matilda, growing tired of play,
And finding she was left alone,
Went tiptoe to the telephone
And summoned the immediate aid
Of London's noble fire-brigade.

Within an hour the gallant band
Were pouring in on every hand,
From Putney, Hackney Downs, and Bow
With courage high and hearts a-glow
They galloped, roaring through the town,
"Matilda's house is burning down!"
Inspired by British cheers and loud
Proceeding from the frenzied crowd,
They ran their ladders through a score
Of windows on the ballroom floor;
And took peculiar pains to souse
The pictures up and down the house,

Until Matilda's Aunt succeeded
In showing them they were not needed;
And even then she had to pay
To get the men to go away!
It happened that a few weeks later
Her Aunt was off to the theatre
To see that interesting play
The Second Mrs. Tanqueray,
She had refused to take her niece
To hear this entertaining piece:
A deprivation just and wise
To punish her for telling lies.

That night a fire *did* break out—
You should have heard Matilda shout!
You should have heard her scream and bawl,
And throw the window up and call
To people passing in the street—
(The rapidly increasing heat
Encouraging her to obtain
Their confidence)—but all in vain!
For every time she shouted "Fire!"
They only answered "Little liar!"
And therefore when her Aunt returned,
Matilda, and the house, were burned.

For the Love of a Man

from

THE CALL OF THE WILD

by

JACK LONDON

The men in the Eldorado Saloon were boasting of their favorite sled dogs. "My dog can start a sled with a load of five hundred pounds and walk off with it," said one. Another man bragged that his dog could pull six hundred pounds.

Matthewson, the richest of the miners, claimed seven hundred pounds for his dog.

John Thornton boasted, "My dog Buck can start a sled with a thousand pounds. He's the best in Alaska."

"Can he break it out of the ice and pull it a hundred yards?" asked Matthewson.

"Buck can do it," John Thornton said coolly.

"Well, I've got a thousand dollars that says he can't," Matthewson stated slowly, so that all could hear. So saying, he slammed a sack of gold dust down on the bar.

Nobody spoke.

John Thornton's bluff, if it was a bluff, had been called. He could feel a flush of warm blood creeping up his face.

His tongue had tricked him, boasting about his dog.
He did not know if Buck could pull a thousand pounds.
Half a ton! The thought of it frightened him.

Maybe Buck could do it, but he had never asked so
much of his dog.

He could feel the eyes of all the men in the saloon
fixed upon him, waiting to see if he would back down
on his boast.

"I've got a sled standing outside now," Matthewson
went on. "It has twenty sacks of flour on it, and they
weigh fifty pounds each. It's on the street right in front
of the door. I'll unhitch my dogs, and you can hitch up
Buck."

John Thornton did not reply. He did not know what to say. He didn't have a sack of gold dust worth a thousand dollars. He would have to borrow money from a friend, just to match Matthewson's bet.

Thornton's eyes traveled from face to face until he spotted an old friend, Jim O'Brien.

"Jim, can you lend me a thousand?" he asked, almost in a whisper.

"Sure," said O'Brien, thumping down a sack of his gold dust by the side of Matthewson's. "Though it's little faith I'm having, John, that the beast can do the trick."

All the men from the Eldorado Saloon emptied into the street to see the test. Matthewson's sled, loaded with the thousand pounds of flour, had been standing for a couple of hours. In the sixty-below-zero cold, the sled's runners had frozen fast to the hard, packed snow.

Matthewson's team of ten dogs was unhitched, and Buck was harnessed to the sled. Buck had caught the excitement in the air, and he felt that in some way he must do a great thing for John Thornton.

Thornton knelt down by Buck's side. He took the dog's head in his two hands and rested cheek on cheek. He did not playfully shake him or murmur soft words to him, but he whispered in his ear, "As you love me, Buck. As you love me."

As John Thornton got to his feet, Buck seized his mittened hand between his jaws, pressed it with his teeth, and let go slowly. It was the answer, in terms, not of speech, but of love.

Thornton stepped well back. "Now, Buck," he said.

Buck tightened the traces, then slacked them for a matter of several inches. It was the way he had learned.

"Gee!" Thornton's voice rang out, sharp in the tense silence.

Buck swung to the right, ending the movement in a jarring plunge. The load quivered, and from under the runners of the sled arose a crisp crackling of ice.

"Haw!" Thornton commanded.

Now Buck swung to the left. The crackling turned into a snapping. The sled was broken out of the ice.

Men were holding their breath as they watched.

"Now, MUSH!" Thornton's command cracked out like a pistol shot.

Buck threw himself forward, tightening the traces with a jarring lunge. His whole body was gathered together in the giant effort. His great chest was low to the ground, and his head was forward and down while his nails were clawing the hard, packed snow. The sled swayed and trembled, half starting forward.

One of Buck's feet slipped, and one man groaned aloud. Then the sled lurched ahead, seeming to jerk forward and then stop, though it never really came to a dead stop again. Half an inch . . . an inch . . . two inches. The jerks were fewer. The sled was moving now. It was picking up speed.

Men gasped and began to breathe again, not knowing that for a moment they had stopped breathing.

Thornton was behind Buck, talking to him, praising him. The hundred yards had been marked off, and as

the dog neared the pile of wood that marked the end, a cheer began to grow and grow. It burst into a roar as Buck passed the wood and stopped at Thornton's command.

Everyone was shouting, even Matthewson. Hats and mittens were flying in the air. Men were shaking hands, it did not matter with whom, and bubbling over with excitement.

But John Thornton fell on his knees beside Buck. Head was against head, and he was whispering to his dog. Thornton's eyes were wet. The tears were streaming frankly down his cheeks.

Buck seized Thornton's hand in his teeth. Thornton shook him back and forth.

As if moved by something they all understood, the men drew back and kept their distance. They had the good sense not to interrupt what was going on between this man and the dog who loved him.

The Cremation of Sam McGee

by

ROBERT W. SERVICE

There are strange things done in the midnight sun
By the men who moil for gold;
The Arctic trails have their secret tales
That would make your blood run cold.
The Northern Lights have seen queer sights,
But the queerest they ever did see
Was that night on the marge of Lake Lebarge
I cremated Sam McGee.

Now Sam McGee was from Tennessee,
     where the cotton blooms and blows.
Why he left his home in the South to roam
     'round the Pole, God only knows.
He was always cold, but the land of gold
     seemed to hold him like a spell,
Though he'd often say in his homely way
     that he'd sooner live in hell.

On a Christmas Day we were mushing our way
     over the Dawson trail.
Talk of your cold! Through the parka's fold
     it stabbed like a driven nail.
If our eyes we'd close, then the lashes froze
     till sometimes we couldn't see.
It wasn't much fun, but the only one
     to whimper was Sam McGee.

And that very night, as we lay packed tight
      in our robes beneath the snow,
And the dogs were fed, and the stars o'erhead
      were dancing heel and toe,
He turned to me, and "Cap," says he,
      "I'll cash in this trip, I guess;
And if I do, I'm asking that you
      won't refuse my last request."

75

Well, he seemed so low that I couldn't say no;
   then he says with a sort of moan:
"It's the cursed cold, and it's got right hold
   till I'm chilled clean through to the bone.
Yet 'taint being dead—it's my awful dread
   of the icy grave that pains;
So I want you to swear that, foul or fair,
   you'll cremate my last remains."

A pal's last need is a thing to heed,
   so I swore I would not fail;
And we started on at the streak of dawn;
   but God! he looked ghastly pale.
He crouched on the sleigh, and he raved all day
   of his home in Tennessee;
And before nightfall a corpse was all
   that was left of Sam McGee.

There wasn't a breath in that land of death,
   and I hurried, horror-driven,
With a corpse half-hid that I couldn't get rid,
   because of a promise given;
It was lashed to the sleigh, and it seemed to say:
   "You may tax your brawn and brains,
But you promised true, and it's up to you
   to cremate these last remains."

Now a promise made is a debt unpaid,
      and the trail has its own stern code.
In the days to come, though my lips were dumb,
      in my heart how I cursed that load.
In the long, long night, by the lone firelight,
      while the Huskies, round in a ring,
Howled out their woes to the homeless snows—
      O God! how I loathed the thing.

And every day that quiet clay
        seemed to heavy and heavier grow;
And on I went, though the dogs were spent
        and the grub was getting low;
The trail was bad, and I felt half mad,
        but I swore I would not give in;
And I'd often sing to the hateful thing,
        and it harkened with a grin.

Till I came to the marge of Lake Lebarge
        and a derelict there lay;
It was jammed in the ice, but I saw in a trice
        it was called the *Alice May*.
And I looked at it, and I thought a bit,
        and I looked at my frozen chum;
Then "Here," said I, with a sudden cry,
        "is my cre-ma-to-re-um."

Some planks I tore from the cabin floor,
        and I lit the boiler fire;
Some coal I found that was lying around,
        and I heaped the fuel higher;
The flames just soared, and the furnace roared—
        such a blaze you seldom see;
And I burrowed a hole in the glowing coal,
        and I stuffed in Sam McGee.

Then I made a hike, for I didn't like
        to hear him sizzle so;
And the heavens scowled, and the Huskies howled,
        and the wind began to blow.
It was icy cold, but the hot sweat rolled
        down my cheeks, and I don't know why;
And the greasy smoke in an inky cloak
        went streaking down the sky.

I do not know how long in the snow
      I wrestled with grisly fear;
But the stars came out and they danced about
      ere again I ventured near;
I was sick with dread, but I bravely said:
      "I'll just take a peep inside.
I guess he's cooked, and it's time I looked";
      . . . then the door I opened wide.

And there sat Sam, looking cool and calm,
      in the heart of the furnace roar;
And he wore a smile you could see a mile,
      and he said: "Please close that door.
It's fine in here, but I greatly fear
      you'll let in the cold and storm—
Since I left Plumtree down in Tennessee,
      it's the first time I've been warm."

There are strange things done in the midnight sun
By the men who moil for gold;
The Arctic trails have their secret tales
That would make your blood run cold;
The Northern Lights have seen queer sights,
But the queerest they ever did see
Was that night on the marge of Lake Lebarge
I cremated Sam McGee.

UNIT TWO

Here and There, Then and Now

The Adventure of the Dancing Men

by

SIR ARTHUR CONAN DOYLE

herlock Holmes tossed a sheet of paper upon the table. "What do you make of this, Watson?" he asked me.

I looked at the row of stick figures on the paper. "Why, Holmes, it is a child's drawing."

"Oh, that's your idea, is it?" he said, with a gleam of amusement in his eyes.

"What else could it be?" I asked.

"That is what Mr. Hilton Cubitt of Riding Thorp Manor, Norfolk, is very anxious to know. This little puzzle came by mail, and he was to follow by the next train to tell me why it troubles him. There's a ring at the bell, Watson. I should not be very much surprised if this were he."

A heavy step was heard upon the stairs of our house on Baker Street. An instant later there entered a tall man whose clear eyes and ruddy cheeks told of a life lived far from the fogs of London. He seemed to bring a whiff of his fresh, east-coast country air with him.

After shaking hands with each of us, he glanced at the table and spotted the paper with the strange little dancing men on it.

"Well, Mr. Holmes, what do you make of this?" he asked. "I was told that you are fond of puzzles. I don't think you could find a stranger puzzle than that. I sent it on ahead so that you might have time to study it before I came."

"At first sight it would appear to be just some childish drawings," said Holmes. "Why should you attach any importance to it?"

"I never should, Mr. Holmes. But my wife does. It is frightening her to death. She says nothing, but I can see terror in her eyes. That is why I want to get to the bottom of the matter."

Holmes held up the paper. It was a page torn from a notebook. The markings were done in pencil, and ran in this way.

He examined it for some time, and then, folding it carefully, he placed it in his pocket.

"This promises to be a most interesting case," said Sherlock Holmes. "Tell me the background, Mr. Hilton Cubitt."

"I suppose I should begin with my marriage last year," said our visitor. "I spend most of my time at my country home. My people have been at Riding Thorp for five centuries. But last year I came up to London for a month and stayed at a boarding house in Russell Square. There was a young American lady staying there too—Elsie Patrick. Before my month was up, I was as much in love as a man could be. We were quietly married in London. Then we returned to my manor in Norfolk as a wedded couple."

He paused, clasping and unclasping his great strong hands. "You'll think it mad, Mr. Holmes, that a man of a fine old family should marry a wife in this way, knowing nothing of her past or of her people. But if you saw her and knew her, it would help you to understand."

Holmes nodded.

"Before Elsie would marry me, she told me, 'I have known some awful people in my life. I wish to forget all about those people. I would rather never talk about the past because it is very painful to me. If you take me, Hilton, you will take a woman who has done nothing that she needs to be ashamed of. But you will have to be content with my word for it. You must allow me to be silent about all that passed up to the time when I became yours.'

87

"I told her that I would take her on her own terms, and I have been as good as my word. We have been married for a year now, and have been very happy. But about a month ago I saw the first signs of trouble. One day my wife received a letter from America. She turned deadly white as she read the letter. Then she threw it into the fire."

"You asked her no questions about it?" Holmes inquired.

"A promise is a promise," said Mr. Cubitt. "I asked nothing. But my poor wife has not known an easy hour from that moment. There is always a look of fear upon her face. She would do better to trust me. She would find that I was her best friend. But until she speaks, I am honor bound not to press her for answers. I am concerned, yes, but I know that Elsie is a good woman. Mind you, Mr. Holmes, whatever trouble there may have been in her past, I am sure it was no fault of hers. Before she married me, she knew that there is not a man in England who ranks his family honor more highly than I do. She would never bring any stain upon it—of that I am sure."

As I listened to Mr. Cubitt, I hoped he was right.

"Well, now I come to the strange part of my story," he went on. "About a week ago I found on one of the window sills a number of little dancing figures, like the ones upon the paper. They were scribbled with chalk. I thought the stable boy had drawn them, but the lad swore he knew nothing about it. I had them washed out, and I only mentioned the matter to my wife afterward.

"To my surprise, she begged me if any more came to

let her see them. Yesterday, I found this paper in the garden. I showed it to Elsie, and down she dropped in a dead faint. Since then she has walked around like a woman in a dream, with terror in her eyes. So I wrote and sent the paper to you, Mr. Holmes. It was not a thing that I could take to the police, for they would have laughed at me."

Sherlock Holmes had listened to the whole story in silence. Now he said, "Don't you think, Mr. Cubitt, that your best plan would be to ask your wife directly to share her secret with you?"

Hilton Cubitt shook his head.

"A promise is a promise, Mr. Holmes," he said. "I will not ask Elsie to tell me anything. But I will try to protect her from whatever it is that is frightening her. So I have come to you."

"Then I will try to help you with all my heart," said Holmes. "First, have you noticed any strangers in your neighborhood?"

"No, but there may be some. We have some inns not very far away. And the farmers sometimes take in lodgers."

Holmes took the paper from his pocket and looked at it again. "These little drawings carry some meaning. But this sample is so short that I can do nothing with it. When you return home, keep a keen lookout. Make an exact copy of any new dancing men that may appear."

Hilton Cubitt promised to do so, shook hands with us, and left.

In the next few days, I saw Sherlock Holmes take out

the slip of paper and study the odd drawings a number of times. But Holmes said nothing further about them until Hilton Cubitt called on us again, about two weeks later.

Mr. Cubitt was looking worried, with tired eyes and lined forehead. "It's getting on my nerves, this business, Mr. Holmes," he said as he sank into an armchair. "It's bad enough to feel that someone unseen, unknown, has some kind of design upon you. But when you know that it is just killing your wife by inches, then it becomes too much to bear."

"Has she said anything yet?" asked Holmes.

"No, but there have been times when the poor girl has wanted to speak, has come close, but yet could not quite bring herself to take the plunge. I have tried to help her. But I did not succeed. Elsie has spoken about my old family, and our pride and honor, and I felt it was leading to the point. But somehow it turned off before we got there."

"But you have found out something for yourself?"

"A good deal, Mr. Holmes," said Hilton Cubitt. "I have some fresh dancing men pictures for you. And, what is more important, I have seen the fellow."

"What! The man who draws them?"

"Yes, I saw him at his work. But let me tell you everything in order." Hilton Cubitt unfolded three papers and laid them on the table. "When I got back after my visit to you, the very first thing I saw the next morning was a fresh crop of dancing men. They had been drawn with chalk on the door. I copied them exactly for you." He pointed to the first paper on the table.

𝌆𝌆 𝌆𝌆𝌆𝌆𝌆𝌆

"Fine!" said Holmes. "And then?"

"After I made the copy for you, I rubbed out the marks. But two mornings later, a new drawing appeared." He pointed to the second paper on the table. "Here is my copy. This very same message was repeated three mornings later."

𝌆𝌆𝌆𝌆 𝌆𝌆𝌆𝌆𝌆

Holmes rubbed his hands and chuckled. "More to work with," he said.

"After that," Hilton Cubitt went on, "I decided to sit up the next night and lie in wait for whoever was drawing these dancing men. I got my gun and stayed by the window in the study, which overlooks the lawn. It was dark, except for the moonlight outside, when I heard steps behind me. There was my wife in her dressing gown. She begged me to come to bed. I told her frankly that I wished to see who it was that played such tricks upon us.

"She said, 'If it really annoys you, Hilton, we might go and travel, you and I, and get away from all this. We can discuss it in the morning.'

"Suddenly, as she spoke, I saw her face grow whiter yet in the moonlight. Her hand tightened upon my shoulder. A man was moving in the shadows, near the

91

door. Seizing my gun, I started to rush out, when my
wife threw her arms around me and held me back. I tried
to throw her off, but she clung to me, stiff with fear.

"By the time I got outside, the man was gone. But he
had left his message. There on the door again was the
same line of dancing men which had appeared twice
before. I ran all over the grounds, but there was no sign
of the fellow anywhere. So I thought he had gotten
away. But he must have been there all the time, for when

I looked again at the door in the morning, there was a new set of pictures under the old line." Hilton Cubitt pointed at the third paper on the table. "It is very short, only five figures. But I made this copy of it for you."

"Tell me," said Holmes, very much excited, "was this on the same line with the other figures?"

"No," said Hilton Cubitt. "It was on another panel of the door. There's the whole case, Mr. Holmes. Now I want your advice on what I should do."

"Leave me these papers, and I think I can soon throw some light upon your case," said Holmes. "If there is another message, please send me a copy at once."

Holmes saw Mr. Hilton Cubitt to the door, and then rushed back to the table. He laid out all the slips with the dancing men drawings. For two hours I watched him as he covered sheet after sheet of paper with letters and figures. Sometimes he was puzzled and would sit for a spell, just staring into space. Other times, he whistled as he seemed to be making progress. At last he sprang from his chair and walked up and down the room, rubbing his hands.

Then he wrote a long telegram upon a cable form. "If my answer to this is as I hope, we shall soon be able to visit Mr. Hilton Cubitt with the solution to his case."

I confess that I was very curious. But I knew that Holmes would tell what he was about only at his own time and in his own way. So I waited, asking no questions.

93

A few mornings later, early deliveries brought both an answer to Holmes's cablegram and another note from Hilton Cubitt. He had sent a copy of this latest line of dancing men.

After quickly reading his cablegram, Holmes bent over the long line of dancing men for some minutes. Then he sprang to his feet, looking greatly concerned.

"We must visit Mr. Hilton Cubitt at once," he said. "Come, Watson. We will catch the next train to Norfolk."

When we reached Riding Thorp Manor and were announced, we were met not by Mr. Hilton Cubitt or his wife. Much to my surprise, we were met by Inspector Martin of the police.

"Why, Mr. Holmes!" the inspector exclaimed. "This crime was only committed at three this morning! The doctor arrived ahead of me, but I have been here only long enough to question the servants. How could you hear of it in London and get to the spot as soon as I?"

Seldom had I seen Holmes so taken aback. "I feared there would be trouble here. I came in the hope of stopping it, but I did not know it had already come to pass. What happened?"

"They are shot, both Mr. Hilton Cubitt and his wife," said the inspector. "She shot him and then herself, or the other way around—so the servants say. He's dead and her life is despaired of. It's a terrible business, and the Cubitts are one of the oldest families in the county."

Holmes's brow grew dark. "I have arrived too late, it seems," he said, almost to himself. Then he threw back his shoulders. "But not too late to see that justice is done."

"I should be proud to feel that we were working together, Mr. Holmes," said Inspector Martin. "I know your record of success in solving puzzling cases. And this case seems puzzling indeed since the servants thought the Cubitts were a close and loving couple."

"I would like to see the servants now and hear their stories of how the shootings happened," said Holmes.

The cook and the housemaid were called. They retold their story clearly enough before all of us. They had been awakened by the sound of a loud explosion, which had been followed a minute later by another one. Together they had hurried down the stairs to the study. Hilton Cubitt lay upon his face, quite dead. Near the window was his wife, horribly wounded. The side of her face was red with blood. The window was shut and fastened upon the inside. The gun lay upon the floor midway between them.

The doctor said Mrs. Cubitt's wound was very serious, perhaps fatal.

Holmes nodded. "I suppose, Doctor, you have not yet recovered the bullet which wounded the lady?"

"I will need to operate to remove the bullet," said the doctor. "But there are still four bullets in the gun. Two have been fired and two people have been shot, so each bullet is accounted for."

"So it might seem," said Holmes. "But how do you account for the bullet which has struck the edge of the window?"

He had turned suddenly, and his long, thin finger was pointing to a hole which had been drilled right through the lower window sill.

"By George!" cried the inspector. "How did you ever see that?"

"Because I looked for it."

"You are certainly right, sir," said the doctor. "Then a third shot has been fired, so a third person must have been present. But who could that have been? And how could he have got away? And how it is that the window came to be shut and fastened?"

"That is the problem we are about to solve," said Holmes. "As to the window, a woman's first instinct would be to shut and fasten it to keep out someone dangerous. And I have reason to believe that someone dangerous came to the house. Also the cook and the maid said they were awakened by a *loud* explosion. That might have been two shots fired at almost the same instant."

"Whom do you suspect, Mr. Holmes?" asked the inspector.

"I'll go into that later," said Holmes. "I think that we can now reconstruct the events of last night and make sure justice is done. But first, I want to know if there is an inn or a farm around here known as 'Elrige's'?"

"A farmer of that name lives some miles away," said the cook.

"Is it a lonely farm?" asked Holmes.

"Very lonely, sir."

"Ask the stable boy to saddle a horse," said Holmes. "I shall want the boy to take a note at once to Elrige's farm."

He took from his pocket the slips of the dancing men. With these in front of him, he worked for some time at the table. Finally, he handed a note to the boy and said, "Give this to Mr. Abe Slaney. Then return at once, and answer no questions."

As the boy left, Holmes set the drawings of the dancing men in order. "Now," he said, "before Mr. Slaney arrives, let me explain about these messages. I have worked before with codes and secret writings. But the first message Mr. Hilton Cubitt brought me was so short that I could not decode it. I could only figure that this symbol

probably stood for the letter E, since E is the most common letter of the alphabet. Of the fifteen symbols in the first message, four were the same.

"In some cases the figure was bearing a flag and in some cases not. So it looked as if the flags were used to break the sentence into words.

"The order of letters after E is by no means well marked. Roughly, T, A, O, I, N, S, H, R, D, and L are the numerical order in which letters occur. But the first four are almost even. So I could not break the code without seeing more messages.

"On Mr. Cubitt's second visit, he brought me two other short sentences and one message which appeared to be a single word. In this single word, there are two E's coming second and fourth in a word of five letters. It might be 'sever' or 'lever' or 'never.' There can be no question that 'never' as a reply is most likely, since the time and place of the word's appearance made me believe it was written by Mrs. Elsie Cubitt. So we can now safely say that the three symbols

stand for N, V, and R.

"It also seemed likely that the messages were coming from someone who had known Elsie before she became Mrs. Hilton Cubitt. The message that was repeated ended in a word that began and ended with E and had three letters between. It had to be some appeal to 'ELSIE.' In this way I got the letters L, S, and I. There were only four letters in the word before ELSIE, and it ended in E. Surely the word must be COME. So now, with the C, O, and M, I could go back to the first

message and work out this much of it.

_M _ERE __E SL_NE_

"Now the first letter has to be A for AM, and only the letter H fits well on the second word to make it HERE. 'AM HERE' would probably be followed by a name. Using my A's, I was able to come up with

AM HERE ABE SLANEY

"Using my letters on the second message, I worked it out in this fashion.

A_ ELRI_ES

"Here I could only make sense by putting T and G for the missing letters, so that I had AT ELRIGES. That had to be the name of some inn or farm where the writer was staying."

Inspector Martin and I listened with great interest to this full and clear account of how Holmes had decoded the messages.

"What did you do then, sir?" asked the inspector.

"I had every reason to suppose that this Abe Slaney was an American who had known Elsie in the past. So I cabled a friend with the New York Police. I asked him if the name Abe Slaney was known to him. Here is the reply, 'One of the most dangerous crooks in the country.' Then Hilton Cubitt sent me the last message from

Slaney. Working with known letters, it took this form.

ELSIE _RE_ARE TO MEET THY GO_

When I added a P to make PREPARE and a D to make
GOD, the message showed me that Slaney was moving
from appeals to threats. So I started here at once with
my friend, Dr. Watson. Sadly, we were too late to prevent
the shooting, but justice will be done.

"My note in Mr. Slaney's code will bring him to us.
In fact, if I am not mistaken, here he is coming up the
drive."

A tall man in a Panama hat was striding up the path
toward the door.

"I think, gentlemen," said Holmes, quietly, "that we
had best take up our positions behind the door."

We waited in silence for a minute—one of those
minutes which one can never forget. Then the door
opened and the man stepped in.

That instant Holmes clapped a pistol to his head and
Martin slipped the handcuffs over his wrists. It was all
done so quickly that the fellow was helpless before he
knew what had happened.

He glared from one to the other of us with blazing
black eyes. Then he burst into a bitter laugh. "Well,
gentlemen, you have the drop on me this time. I seem to
have knocked up against something hard. But I came
here in answer to a note from Mrs. Hilton Cubitt. Don't
tell me she is in on this? Don't tell me she helped set a
trap for me?"

"Mrs. Hilton Cubitt was shot and is at death's door," said Holmes.

The man gave a hoarse cry of grief that rang through the house.

"You're crazy!" he cried. "It was he that was hurt, not she! Who would have hurt little Elsie? I may have threatened her, God forgive me, but I would not have touched a hair of her pretty head. Take it back—you! Say that she is not hurt!"

"She was found badly wounded by the side of her dead husband," said Holmes.

Slaney sank with a deep groan onto the chair and buried his face in his hands.

"If Elsie dies," he cried, "I don't care what becomes of me. Her father pledged her to me years ago. He was boss of our gang. But Elsie couldn't stand the business, so she gave us the slip and got away to London. I think she would have married me if I had left the gang and gone straight. So who was this Englishman that he should come between us?"

He opened one of his hands and looked at the crumpled note he was holding. "Wait a minute," cried Slaney, "you're not trying to scare me over this, are you? If she's hurt as bad as you say, who wrote this note?" He tossed it onto the table.

"I wrote it to bring you here," said Holmes.

"You wrote it? There was no one on earth outside our gang and Elsie who knew the secret code of the dancing men."

"What one man can invent, another can discover," said Holmes. He gave Abe Slaney a grim look. "You said that you loved this lady, but you dogged her and made her life a misery. She ran away from you whom she hated and feared. But you followed her and tried to get her to leave the husband she loved. You have ended by killing a good and kind man and driving his wife to suicide. You will have to answer to the law, Mr. Abe Slaney."

For a minute Slaney was silent. Then he spoke in the quiet voice of despair. "I have nothing to hide now, Mr. Holmes. I wrote Elsie from America, but she wouldn't answer my letters. So I had to come here to reach her. It is true, I tried to coax her away. I knew she read the

103

messages, for once she wrote an answer under one of them. Then my temper got the better of me, and I began to threaten her.

"She sent me a letter then, begging me to go away and saying it would break her heart if any scandal should come upon her husband. She said that she would come down early in the morning, while her husband was asleep, and speak with me at the window if I would go away afterward and leave her in peace. She came down and brought money with her to try to bribe me to go. That made me mad. I grabbed her arm and tried to pull her through the window.

"At that moment, in rushed her husband with a gun in his hand. We were face to face. I held up my gun to scare him off. He fired first and missed me. I fired almost at the same instant, and down he dropped. I made my escape across the garden, and as I went I heard the window shut behind me. That's the whole story, gentlemen, every word of it, and I heard no more until your lad came riding up with the note which made me walk here, into your hands."

Inspector Martin rose and touched the prisoner on the shoulder.

"It is time for us to go," he said.

Holmes and I stood at the window and watched Inspector Martin and Slaney leave. As I turned back, my eye caught the piece of paper which the prisoner had tossed upon the table. It was the note with which Holmes trapped Abe Slaney.

"See if you can read it, Watson," said he with a smile.

It contained no word, but this little line of dancing men.

"If you use the code that I explained," said Holmes, "you will find that it simply means, 'Come here at once.' I knew he would come, since he could not have dreamed that the note was from anyone but the lady."

•   •   •   •

Months later, we heard that Abe Slaney was sent to prison. Of Mrs. Hilton Cubitt, I only know that I have heard she finally recovered, is still a widow, and spends all her time taking care of the poor and her late husband's manor.

A Creed

by

EDWIN MARKHAM

There is a destiny that makes us brothers.
　　None goes his way alone.
All that we send into the lives of others
　　Comes back into our own.

I care not what his temples or his creeds,
　　One thing holds firm and fast—
That into his fateful heap of days and deeds
　　The soul of a man is cast.

Psalm of Life

from the poem by

HENRY WADSWORTH LONGFELLOW

Lives of great men all remind us
We can make our lives sublime,
And, departing, leave behind us
Footprints on the sands of time.

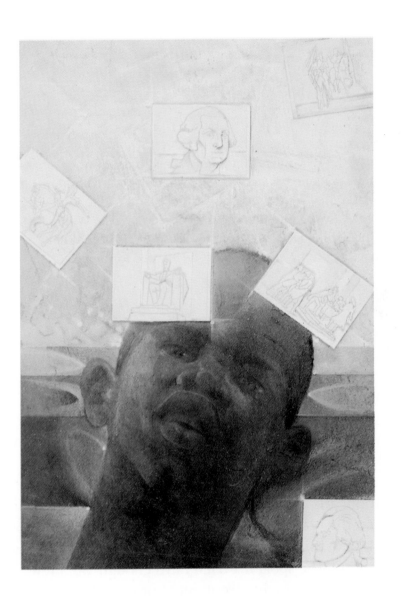

Before Olympic Medals

from

WILMA

by

WILMA RUDOLPH

At the 1960 Olympic Games Wilma Rudolph won three gold medals in track. But when she was a child in Clarksville, Tennessee, she was sickly and had to wear a leg brace. By the time she was a teenager, however, Wilma Rudolph had started winning races. In this part of her autobiography, she tells how she learned to compete.

So, it's 1956 and I'm fifteen, and my life has never been better. I couldn't remember being happier. School was fun then. At Burt High School we were all black. I remember we'd have dance contests every week. I even won a couple of times, but most of my life revolved around track and my family.

As soon as basketball season ended, I had my track stuff on, and I was running. That taste of winning I had gotten the year before never left me. I was serious about track now, thinking deep down inside that maybe I had a future in the sport if I tried hard enough. So a few times I cut classes and went out to practice running.

One day I got a call to report to the principal's office.

I went in, and he said, "Wilma, I know how important running track is to you. I hope you will become a big success at it. Nevertheless, you can't cut classes."

I was, well, mortified. The principal had found me out.

He finally said that if I continued cutting classes, he would have to tell my father, and I knew what that meant. So I stopped. Even so, I was the first girl out there at practice and the last one to leave, I loved it so. We had some playday meets early that season, and I kept on winning all the races I was in. I felt unbeatable.

Then came the big meet at Tuskegee, Alabama. It was the biggest meet of the year. Girls from all over the South were invited down there to run, and the competition was the best for high school kids.

Coach Gray was going to drive us all down to Tuskegee Institute, and I remember we brought our very best dresses since there would be a big dance after the meet. We all piled into his car until there wasn't an inch of empty space left.

All the way down to Alabama, we talked and laughed and had a good time, and Coach Gray would tell us how tough the competition was going to be, especially the girls from Atlanta, Georgia, because they had a lot of black schools down there, and they had these track programs that ran the whole year because of the warm weather. When we got there, all of us were overwhelmed, because that was the first college campus any of us ever saw. We stayed in this big dorm, and I remember just before the first competition, I started getting this nervous feeling that would stay with me for the rest of my running career. Every time before a race, I would get it, this horrible feeling in the pit of my stomach, a combination of nerves and not eating.

When we got to the track, these girls from Georgia really looked like runners, but I paid them no mind because, well, I was a little cocky. I did think I could wipe them out because, after all, I had won every single race I had ever been in up to that point. So what happens? I got wiped out. It was the absolute worst experience of my life. I did not win a single race I ran in, nor did I qualify for anything. I was totally crushed. The girls from Georgia won everything. It was the first time I had ever tasted defeat in track, and it left me a total wreck. I was so despondent that I refused to go to any of the activities that were planned, including the big dance. I can't remember ever being so totally crushed by anything.

On the ride back, I sat in the car and didn't say a word to anybody. I just thought to myself about how much work was ahead of me and how I would like nothing better in the whole world than to come back to Tuskegee the next year and win everything. When I got home, my father knew immediately what had happened, and he didn't say anything. Every time I used to come home after a meet, I would rush into the house all excited and bubble over with, "I won . . . I won." This time I didn't say a word. I just walked in quietly, nodded to my father who was sitting there, and went into my room and unpacked.

After so many easy victories, using natural ability alone, I got a false sense of being unbeatable. But losing

Wilma Rudolph, second from left, with her mother, Blanche, father, Ed, and sister, Charlene

to those girls from Georgia, who knew every trick in the book, that was sobering. It brought me back down to earth, and it made me realize that I couldn't do it on natural ability alone, that there was more to track than just running fast. I also realized it was going to test me as a person—could I come back and win again after being so totally crushed by a defeat?

When I went back to school, I knew I couldn't continue to cut classes to practice or else I'd be in big trouble. So I would fake sickness, tell the teacher that I didn't feel well and could I please go home? They would let me go, and then I would go over to the track and run.

When that stopped working, when they realized that I looked pretty good for being sick all the time, I simply asked them point-blank, "Look, could I cut this class today and go out and run?" Believe it or not, a lot of teachers said, "Okay, Wilma, go, but don't tell anybody."

I ran and ran and ran every day, and I acquired this sense of determination, this sense of spirit that I would never, never give up, no matter what else happened. That day at Tuskegee had a tremendous effect on me inside. That's all I ever thought about. Some days I just wanted to go out and die. I just moped around and felt sorry for myself. Other days I'd go out to the track with fire in my eyes, and imagine myself back at Tuskegee, beating them all. Losing as badly as I did had an impact on my personality. Winning all the time in track had given me confidence; I felt like a winner. But I didn't feel like a winner any more after Tuskegee. My confidence was shattered and I was thinking the only way I could put it all together was to get back the next year and wipe them all out.

But looking back on it all, I realized somewhere along the line that to think that way wasn't necessarily right, that it was kind of extreme. I learned a very big lesson for the rest of my life as well. The lesson was, winning is great, sure, but if you are really going to do something in life, the secret is learning how to lose. Nobody goes undefeated all the time. If you can pick up after a crushing defeat, and go on to win again, you are going to be a champion someday. But if losing destroys you, it's all over. You'll never be able to put it all back together again.

I did, almost right away. There were more playdays scheduled, and I won all the rest of the races I was in the rest of that season. But I never forgot Tuskegee. In fact, I was thinking that anybody who saw me lose so badly at the meet would write me off immediately. I was wrong. One day, right after the track season ended that year, Coach Gray came over to me and he said, "Wilma, Ed Temple, the referee who is the women's track coach at Tennessee State, is going to be coming down to Clarksville to talk with your mother and father."

"What about?" I asked.

"Wilma," he said, "I think he wants you to spend the summer with him at the college, learning the techniques of running."

117

The Runner

by

WALT WHITMAN

On a flat road runs the well-trained runner.
He is lean and sinewy with muscular legs.
He is thinly clothed. He leans forward as he runs,
With lightly closed fists and arms partially raised.

119

Being Reasonable

by

BENJAMIN FRANKLIN

On my first voyage from Boston, the people on board with me set about catching codfish. They hauled up a great many.

I knew that some thinkers considered the killing and eating of fish as murder, since no fish ever had done (or ever could do) any harm to us. Such thinkers were reasonable, fair-minded people. I could not do less than agree with them. So there were times when I refused to eat anything but vegetables.

But I was a great lover of fried fish. When they came hot out of the pan, they smelled delicious. For a little time, I hung in the balance—to eat or not to eat the codfish.

Then I remembered that when those fish were opened, I saw smaller fish taken out of their stomachs. So I thought, "If you eat one another, I don't see why we may not eat you." After that, I dined upon the fried cod very heartily.

It is so convenient to be "reasonable," since it helps one find or make a reason for everything one has a mind to do.

Comments on a Proverb

by

BURR SHAFER

"To tell the truth, Mr. Franklin, we merchants would like a little
less about thrift and more about spending."

Journal

by

RALPH WALDO EMERSON

I like people who can do things. When Edward and I struggled in vain to drag a big calf into the barn, the farm girl put her finger into the calf's mouth, and led him in directly.

Winslow Homer
Weaning the Calf, 1875
Collection of the North Carolina Museum of Art, Raleigh

The Wind and the Sun

from

AESOP'S FABLES

For a long time the Wind had been telling the Sun, "I am far stronger than you." But the Sun just smiled and shook his head. "You are mistaken," he said.

"But I can blow down a tree!" exclaimed the Wind. "You can't!"

"That is true," agreed the Sun, "but still I am stronger than you."

"Prove it!" snapped the Wind.

"Very well," the Sun said quietly. "On the road below us is a man with a coat on. Let's agree that whichever of us can get the coat off the man is the stronger."

"Fine!" said the Wind. "When I blow with all my might, I can take the roof off a house. Just watch me take the coat off that man."

The Wind began to blow. The man's coat flapped open, but as the Wind blew harder, the man walked faster and pulled his coat together over his chest. Then the Wind let loose and blew with all his might, trying to tear the coat apart. The man wrapped it around him even more tightly. Finally the Wind had to give up.

Then the Sun came out, shining softly. He poured his warm beams down on the man. In a little while he opened his coat. The Sun warmed the air around him. The man slowed down and shaded his eyes as the Sun rose higher in the sky, beaming kindly and brightly. The man soon felt that it was too hot to walk with his coat on, so he took it off.

Kindness works better than force.

Pioneering by Lake Ontario

from

PICTURES OF CANADA

by

CATHARINE TRAILL

Catharine Traill wrote *Pictures of Canada* as a series of letters between two sisters, Agnes and Ellen Clarence. Agnes Clarence left England with her parents in the early 1800s to settle in Canada, but her sister Ellen had to stay behind because of poor health. Agnes's letters to Ellen tell of life as a settler in a little farming town near Lake Ontario.

April 22, 1826

My dear sister Ellen,

Now I sit down again to write to you, in hopes that you will soon be well enough to join the family here in Canada. Earlier this year the snow lay for eight weeks to the depth of many feet. It was a fine season for sleighing, which is delightful. As you glide along the frozen surface, the bells on the necks of the horses make a pretty jingling noise, and when you get used to the sound, you do not like to travel without it.

In winter you cannot go a mile from home without seeing twenty or more other sleighs, parties of gentlemen and ladies ice-skating, and children sliding. The farmers choose this time to travel to market and to carry their corn to the mill to be ground into flour. We may travel sixty miles in a sleigh with one pair of horses without suffering from the cold because we wrap up so closely in our plaids and furs, leaving only our faces uncovered.

Harrison.

127

Our fireside presents a scene indoors that is just as cheery as the outdoors. The hearth is piled high with blazing logs of pine. Sometimes we have our neighbors, the Hamiltons, over for the evening. Then Frank Hamilton plays on the flute for us and we sing, or one of us reads aloud while the rest play chess or draw.

When the hour of supper comes, Mamma and I lay the cloth on the table. Then we have a simple meal of bread, dried venison, butter, honey, apples, and cranberry tarts. Such is our supper, and who could wish for more?

Now that the weather is milder, the family is even busier. I usually rise at five o'clock. While Papa is milking the cows, I am in the dairy taking the cream off the milk and making the cheese. Twice a week we make butter.

As soon as the work in the dairy is done, I fill my apron with corn and go to my poultry yard. There I am greeted by fowls of all sorts and sizes, eager to receive their breakfasts from my hand. After I have gathered all the eggs I can find, I give my two weaning calves, Blackberry and Strawberry, their warmed milk. Then I return to the house for my breakfast.

Once a week I help Mamma bake. Here in Canada we make the household bread from a mixture of rye and maize flour, and new milk. It is nicer than the best English bread I ever tasted. My cakes and puddings bring me praise from Papa, and I make all the pastry. I plan to preserve a great deal of fruit this summer, since we have a good store of maple sugar.

Papa hired a party of Indians to make the sugar for us, as they know far more than we settlers do about refining it. Some of our neighbors killed their maple trees when they tried to collect the sap. But the Indians know how to get the sap without damaging the tree.

They make a hole in the trunk. Into the hole they insert a tube of elderwood. The sap flows through the tube into the troughs below. At the end of each day the Indians pour the sap into a large pot and light a fire around it. Then they boil and stir the sap until it thickens.

Two gallons of sap produce one pound of sugar. From our two hundred and sixty maple trees, the Indians produced a goodly stock of syrup and sugar, more than I will need for my fruit preserves.

I often walked with Papa and Mamma into the woods to visit the Indians while they were making the sugar. Among the Indians was one old man with whom I formed quite a friendship. He used to lift me over the fallen timbers and place me near the fire where he would stir the sap.

This old Indian's name was Hawk Head. He said that long ago, when he was young and strong, a missionary had stayed with his tribe for a year. The missionary had started to teach him to read, but he told me that he no longer remembered what he had learned.

"Young lady," he said to me. "Hawk Head has grown old. Now his eyes are dim. He has seen his children, to the third generation, rise up before him, and he expects soon to be called away. But Hawk Head would be glad to see his children taught, as he was taught."

I told him I would like to teach a class in the evening for the children of his tribe. He said he would speak to his people about it. I soon had fourteen Indian children as my students. Some of their mothers came with them, so that they too might learn to read. Quickly the numbers grew to twenty-five.

Then our neighbors the Hamiltons said they would like to help me. We plan to set up a regular school for the Indian children and the children of the Irish peasants who have settled nearby. You do not know, my dear sister Ellen, what real and heartfelt pleasure I take in teaching these people, who are so eager to learn.

We are prospering, and we want all others around us to prosper also. Our livestock has increased a great deal since last year. We have a flock of ten young lambs, as white as snow. We also have fifteen pigs and two calves, and we bought a yoke of oxen.

Here in Canada, farmers live on their own produce. It consists of pork, mutton, venison, poultry, game, fish, bread, cakes of Indian corn, milk, eggs, and sugar.

We make our own candles and soap. So you see, my dear sister, that even if we don't have the luxuries of life, we do have all that is really needed for comfort.

Papa intends to build a sawmill, which can be worked by the little stream of water that flows through our grounds. The woods are nearby, so we have plenty of timber.

Last year, the woods caught fire, because of the extreme dryness of the season. When the forest takes fire, it presents a frightening scene. The flames rush to the tops of the trees, roaring, crackling, crashing, and red and yellow smoke waves about the burning woods.

When the fire is over, the forest is a sad sight. Instead of fresh green trees, waving in the winds, you see only black branchless trunks. Ashes cover the once-flowery ground. All is dark and dismal, that was lately so fresh and lovely.

But even a forest fire is not without its benefits. The woods are freed, in the course of a few hours, from the crowding of timber which shuts out the sunlight.

The ashes make the ground ripe for new growth. And the fine Canadian forest soon starts to build itself back. This is a thriving land.

Papa and all the other Canadian settlers from England say that taxes are low here. For every acre of farmland, the settler pays one penny. Besides this, we pay for the upkeep of our roads, or we gladly give a certain number of days a year to work on the roads. It is in the interest of all of us to improve the roads as much as we can.

Sometimes we get a visit from travelers who are using those roads. As is the custom of the country, we set before all strangers the best food the house can offer. We take care of their horses, and we give them a place to sleep for as long as they need. Then we speed them on their journey, wishing them health.

At this time, we have with us a lady who is traveling to the city of New York. She has kindly offered to forward whatever our family might wish to send to England, by the first ship that sails from New York. Since she is leaving soon, I must close this letter so that she can carry it with her to New York and forward it to you.

Love and good wishes from your fond sister,
Agnes Clarence

Stopping by Woods on a Snowy Evening

by

ROBERT FROST

Whose woods these are I think I know.
His house is in the village though;
He will not see me stopping here
To watch his woods fill up with snow.

My little horse must think it queer
To stop without a farmhouse near
Between the woods and frozen lake
The darkest evening of the year.

He gives his harness bells a shake
To ask if there is some mistake.
The only other sound's the sweep
Of easy wind and downy flake.

The woods are lovely, dark and deep,
But I have promises to keep,
And miles to go before I sleep,
And miles to go before I sleep.

Give Me Liberty or Give Me Death

by

PATRICK HENRY

Howard Pyle
The Battle of Bunker Hill
Delaware Art Museum

entlemen may cry peace, peace—but there is no peace. The war is actually begun! The next gale that sweeps down from the north will bring to our ears the clash of resounding arms. Our brethren are already in the field. Why stand we here idle?

Is life so dear, or peace so sweet, as to be purchased at the price of chains and slavery? Forbid it, Almighty God! I know not what course others may take; but as for me, give me liberty or give me death!

These Are the Times That Try Men's Souls

from

THE AMERICAN CRISIS

by

THOMAS PAINE

These are the times that try men's souls. The summer soldier and the sunshine patriot will, in this crisis, shrink from the service of their country. But he that stands *now* deserves the love and thanks of man and woman. Tyranny is not easily conquered. Yet we have this consolation with us—that the harder the conflict, the more glorious the triumph.

Gettysburg Address

by

ABRAHAM LINCOLN

Fourscore and seven years ago, our fathers brought forth upon this continent a new nation, conceived in liberty, and dedicated to the proposition that all men are created equal. Now we are engaged in a great civil war, testing whether that nation, or any nation so conceived and so dedicated, can long endure.

We are met on a great battlefield of that war. We have come to dedicate a portion of that field as a final resting place for those who here gave their lives that this nation might live.

It is altogether fitting and proper that we should do this. But in a larger sense we cannot dedicate, we cannot consecrate, we cannot hallow this ground. The brave men, living and dead, who struggled here, have consecrated it far above our poor power to add or detract. The world will little note, nor long remember, what we say here. But it can never forget what they did here.

It is for us, the living, rather to be dedicated here to the unfinished work which they who fought here have thus far so nobly advanced. It is rather for us to be here

dedicated to the great task remaining before us, that
from these honored dead we take increased devotion to
that cause for which they gave the last full measure of
devotion; that we here highly resolve that these dead

shall not have died in vain; that this nation, under God, shall have a new birth of freedom; and that government of the people, by the people, and for the people, shall not perish from the earth.

Etched across the Pages of History

from

LETTER FROM A BIRMINGHAM JAIL

by

MARTIN LUTHER KING, JR.

We were here before the mighty words of the Declaration of Independence were etched across the pages of history. Our forebears labored without wages. They made cotton "king." And yet out of a bottomless vitality, they continued to thrive and develop. If the cruelties of slavery could not stop us, the opposition we now face will surely fail.

Mother to Son

by

LANGSTON HUGHES

Well, son, I'll tell you:
Life for me ain't been no crystal stair.
It's had tacks in it,
And splinters,
And boards torn up,
And places with no carpet on the floor—
Bare.
But all the time
I'se been a-climbin' on,
And reachin' landin's,
And turnin' corners,
And sometimes goin' in the dark
Where there ain't been no light.
So boy, don't you turn back.
Don't you set down on the steps
'Cause you finds it's kinder hard.
Don't you fall now—
For I'se still goin', honey,
I'se still climbin',
And life for me ain't been no crystal stair.

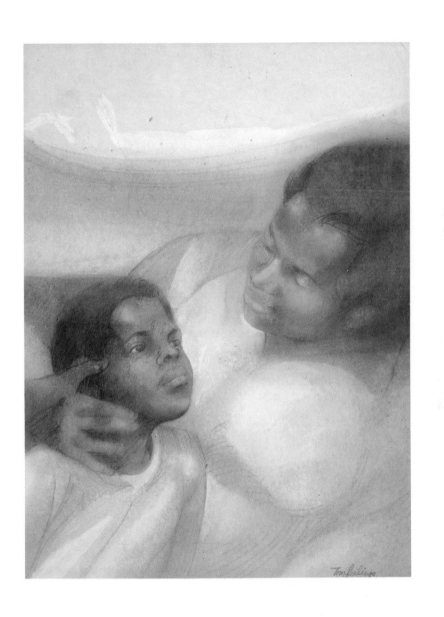

My Little Son

from the

MAKAH

My little son,
you will put a whale harpoon
and a sealing spear into your canoe,
not knowing what use you will make of them.

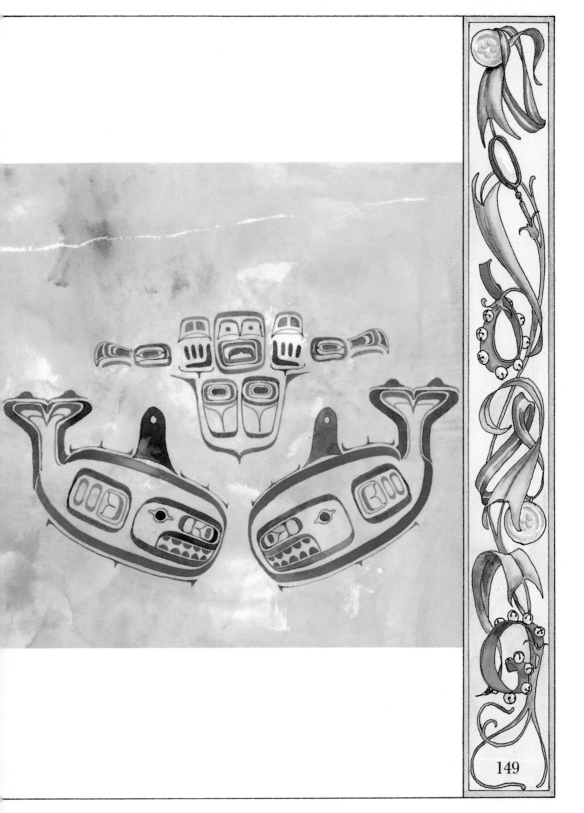

A Runaway

by

SAIGYŌ HOSHI

My pony's tracks
Are buried deep in the snow.
Those from whom I fled,
Left far behind, will wonder
Which way they ought to go.

The Road Not Taken

by

ROBERT FROST

Two roads diverged in a yellow wood,
And sorry I could not travel both
And be one traveler, long I stood
And looked down one as far as I could
To where it bent in the undergrowth;

Then took the other, as just as fair,
And having perhaps a better claim,
Because it was grassy and wanted wear;
Though as for that the passing there
Had worn them really about the same.

And both that morning equally lay
In leaves no steps had trodden black.
Oh, I kept the first for another day!
Yet knowing how way leads on to way,
I doubted if I should ever come back.

I shall be telling this with a sigh
Somewhere ages and ages hence:
Two roads diverged in a wood, and I—
I took the one less traveled by,
And that has made all the difference.

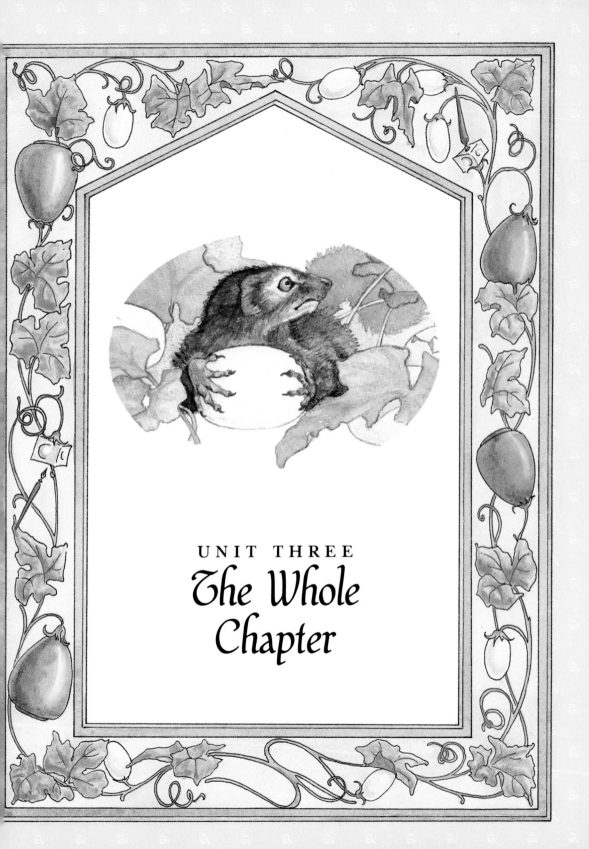

UNIT THREE

The Whole Chapter

Rikki-Tikki-Tavi

from

THE JUNGLE BOOK

by

RUDYARD KIPLING

This is the story of the great fight that Rikki-tikki-tavi fought single-handed against the deadly cobra snakes, to defend Teddy's family. Rikki-tikki-tavi was a mongoose, rather like a little cat in his fur and tail, but quite like a weasel in his head and habits. His war-cry, as he dashed through the long grasses near the English settlement in India, was *"Rikk-tikk-tikki."*

One day a high summer flood washed him out of the burrow where he lived with his father and mother, and carried him, kicking and choking, down a roadside ditch. He found a little wisp of grass floating there and hung on to it till he lost his senses.

When he opened his eyes again, he was lying in the hot sun on the middle of a garden path, very still indeed.

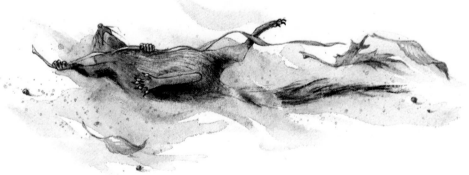

A boy was saying, "Here's a dead mongoose. Let's have a funeral for him."

"No, let's take him in and dry him," said the boy's mother. "Maybe he isn't really dead."

They took him into the house where a big man picked him up between his finger and thumb. "He's not dead, but half choked," said the man.

So they wrapped him in cotton, and warmed him. At last he opened his eyes and shook himself.

"Don't frighten him," said the big man. "We'll see what he'll do."

It is the hardest thing in the world to frighten a mongoose, because he is eaten up from nose to tail with curiosity. Rikki-tikki-tavi looked at the cotton, decided it was not good to eat, and ran all round the table. Then he sat up, put his fur in order, and jumped on the boy's shoulder.

"Don't be frightened, Teddy," said his father. "That's his way of making friends."

"Let's give him something to eat," said Teddy's father.

They gave him a little piece of raw meat. Rikki-tikki-tavi liked it very much. When he was finished, he went out into the sunshine. Then he felt better. "There are lots of things to find out about in this house," he said to himself. "I shall certainly stay and explore."

He spent all that day running about the house. He nearly drowned himself in the bathtub. He put his nose into the ink on the writing table. At nightfall he went into Teddy's room to watch how kerosene lamps were lighted.

When Teddy went to bed, Rikki-tikki-tavi climbed up on his covers, but he was restless. He had to get up and look into every noise he heard, and find out what made it.

Teddy's mother and father came in, the last thing, to look at their son. Rikki-tikki-tavi was awake on the boy's pillow.

"I don't like that," said Teddy's mother. "He may bite Teddy."

"He'll do no such thing," said the father. "Teddy's safer with that little mongoose than if he had a watchdog with him. If a snake came into this room now—"

But Teddy's mother wouldn't think of anything so awful.

Early in the morning, Rikki-tikki-tavi went out into the garden to see what was to be seen. He ran up and down the paths until he heard very sad voices in a bush.

It was Darzee, a little bird, and his wife. They had made a beautiful nest and filled it with cotton, but as they sat on it, they were crying.

"What is the matter?" asked Rikki-tikki-tavi.

"We are very sad," said Darzee. "One of our babies fell out of the nest yesterday, and Nag ate him."

"H'm!" said Rikki. "That is very sad—but I am a stranger here. Who is Nag?"

The two birds only cowered down in their nest without answering, for from the thick grass there came a low hiss. It was a horrid cold sound that made Rikki jump back in a flash.

Then inch by inch out of the grass rose up the head of Nag, the huge king cobra. He was five feet long from tongue to tail. When he had lifted one third of himself clear of the ground, he stayed swaying to and fro, and he looked at Rikki with his wicked snake's eyes.

"Who is Nag?" said he, spreading out his hood. "*I* am Nag. Look, and tremble in fear!"

Rikki felt fear for a moment, but it is impossible for a mongoose to stay fearful for any length of time. Though Rikki had never met a live cobra before, he remembered that his mother had fed him on dead ones. He knew that it was a grown mongoose's business in life to fight and eat snakes.

Nag knew that too, and at the bottom of his cold heart, he was afraid.

"Well," said Rikki-tikki-tavi. "Do you think it is right for you to eat baby birds that fall out of a nest?"

Nag was thinking to himself, and watching the least little movement in the grass behind Rikki. He knew that mongooses in the garden meant death sooner or later for him and his family. Nag wanted to get Rikki off his

guard. So he dropped his head a little, and put it on one side.

"Let us talk," he said. "You eat eggs. Why should not I eat birds?"

"Behind you! Look behind you!" sang Darzee.

Rikki-tikki-tavi knew better than to waste time in staring. He jumped up in the air as high as he could go. Just under him whizzed the head of Nagaina, Nag's wicked wife. She had crept up behind him as he was talking, to make an end of him.

He heard her angry hiss as her stroke missed. Then he came down almost across her back. If he had been

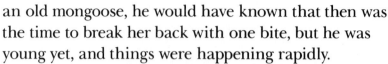

an old mongoose, he would have known that then was the time to break her back with one bite, but he was young yet, and things were happening rapidly.

He bit, indeed! But he did not bite long enough before he jumped clear, leaving Nagaina torn and angry. At once, she and Nag disappeared into the grass.

Rikki-tikki-tavi did not care to follow them, for he did not feel sure that he could manage two snakes at once, so he sat down to think about his battle. He knew he was just a young mongoose, and he felt quite pleased with himself to think that he had managed to escape a blow from behind. He had done well! When Teddy came running down the path, Rikki-tikki-tavi was ready to be petted.

But just as Teddy was stooping, something moved in the dust. A tiny voice threatened, "Be careful. I am death!"

It was the voice of Karait, the dusty brown snake that lies by choice on the dusty earth. His bite is as dangerous as the cobra's, but he is so small that nobody thinks of him, and so he does more harm to people.

Rikki-tikki-tavi's eyes grew red and hot. He danced up to Karait the snake with the rocking, swaying motion of a mongoose. That moment, he was doing a much more dangerous thing than fighting Nag the cobra. No eye can follow the motion of a snake's head when it strikes. But Nag's strike could not be as quick as that of the small snake.

The dusty brown snake could turn so quickly that unless Rikki bit him close to the back of the head, he would get the return stroke in his eye or lip. But Rikki did not stop to think of that. His eyes were red and he rocked back and forth, looking for a good place to hold.

Karait struck out at him. Rikki jumped sideways and tried to run in, but the wicked little dusty brown head lashed within a fraction of his shoulder. He had to jump over the body, and the head of the snake followed close at his heels.

Teddy shouted to the house. "Oh, look here! Our mongoose is fighting a snake!"

Rikki-tikki-tavi heard a scream from Teddy's mother. His father ran out with a stick. But by the time he came up, the snake had lashed out once too far. Rikki had sprung, jumped on the snake's back, bitten as high up the back as he could get hold, and rolled away. That bite struck true.

Just as Rikki-tikki-tavi was starting to eat him up from the tail, he remembered that a full meal makes a slow mongoose. If he wanted all his quickness ready, he must keep himself thin.

He went away for a dust bath under the bushes while Teddy's father beat the dead snake with a stick. Then Teddy's mother picked up Rikki-tikki and hugged him, crying that he had saved Teddy's life.

That night at dinner, he could have stuffed himself three times over with nice things, but he remembered Nag and Nagaina, the cobras. Though it was very pleasant to be patted and petted, he knew he must be ready. From time to time, he would go off into his long war cry of *"Rikk-tikk-tikki."*

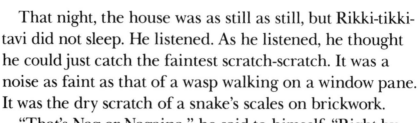

That night, the house was as still as still, but Rikki-tikki-tavi did not sleep. He listened. As he listened, he thought he could just catch the faintest scratch-scratch. It was a noise as faint as that of a wasp walking on a window pane. It was the dry scratch of a snake's scales on brickwork.

"That's Nag or Nagaina," he said to himself. "Right by the house!"

He followed the sound to the bathroom of Teddy's parents. At the bottom of the wall, there was a brick pulled out to make a drain for the bathwater. As Rikki stole in, he heard Nag and Nagaina whispering together outside in the moonlight.

"Kill the man first!" hissed Nagaina. "Then kill the woman and child. When the house is empty of people, the mongoose will go away. Then the garden will be safe for us again and for all snakes after us. As soon as our eggs in the melon bed hatch, our new babies will need room and quiet."

"Yes," said Nag. "I will bite the man and then his wife, and I will bite the child if I can, and come away quietly. Then the house will be empty, so Rikki-tikki-tavi will go."

Rikki-tikki-tavi tingled all over with rage and hatred when he heard this. Then Nag's head came through the opening, and his five feet of cold body followed it. Angry as he was, Rikki was frightened when he saw the full length of the big cobra.

Nag waved to and fro. Then Rikki-tikki heard him drinking from the big water jar that was used to fill the bath. "When the big man comes in to bathe in the morning, I shall strike," said the snake. "Nagaina, do you hear me? I shall wait here in the cool until daytime."

There was no answer from outside, so Rikki-tikki-tavi knew Nagaina had gone away. Nag coiled himself down, coil by coil, round the bottom of the water jar. Rikki-tikki-tavi stayed still as death.

After an hour he began to move, muscle by muscle, toward the jar. Nag the cobra was asleep. Rikki-tikki-tavi looked at his big back, wondering which would be the best place for a good hold. "If I don't break his back at the first jump," said Rikki, "he can still fight. And if he fights—oh, Rikki!"

He looked at the thickness of Nag's neck below the hood, but that was too much for him. A bite near the tail would not work either.

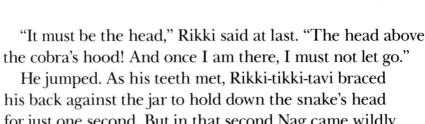

"It must be the head," Rikki said at last. "The head above the cobra's hood! And once I am there, I must not let go."

He jumped. As his teeth met, Rikki-tikki-tavi braced his back against the jar to hold down the snake's head for just one second. But in that second Nag came wildly awake. Then Rikki-tikki-tavi was battered to and fro as a rat is shaken by a dog. To and fro on the floor! Up and down, and round in great circles!

But his eyes were red, and he held on as the cobra's long body whipped over the floor. Nag upset the tin dipper and the soap dish. He banged against the tin side of the bathtub.

As Rikki-tikki-tavi held on, he closed his jaws tighter and tighter. He was sure he would be banged to death, and he wanted to be found with his teeth locked onto the head of the cobra.

He was dizzy, frightened, and felt shaken to pieces when something went off like a clap of thunder just behind him. A hot wind knocked him senseless, and red fire burned the tip ends of his fur. The big man had been awakened by the noise, and he had fired his gun into Nag just below the cobra's hood.

Rikki-tikki-tavi held on with his eyes shut. Now he was quite sure he was dead. But the cobra's head did not move.

In a minute, the big man picked him up and said, "It's the mongoose again, Alice. The little chap has saved *our* lives now."

Then Teddy's mother came in with a very white face and saw what was left of Nag. Rikki-tikki-tavi dragged himself to Teddy's bedroom. He spent the rest of the night shaking himself carefully to find out whether he really was broken into pieces, as he thought.

When morning came, he was still a bit stiff, but well pleased with his doings. "Now I have Nagaina to settle with," thought Rikki. "She will be worse than five Nags, and there's no telling when her eggs in the melon bed will hatch. I could be fighting a garden full of young cobras."

Rikki stole into the melon patch. There he found her eggs, covered with whitish skin instead of shell. He could see the baby cobras curled up inside the skin. He knew that the minute they were hatched, they could each kill a man or a mongoose.

He bit off the tops of the eggs as fast as he could, taking care to crush the young cobras. At last there were only three eggs left. Rikki-tikki-tavi began to chuckle to himself, when he heard Darzee's wife screaming.

"Rikki-tikki-tavi! The man threw out Nag's body. And Nagaina has seen it. She swore that before night the boy of the house would lie still. She has gone onto the porch. Oh, come quickly! She means killing!"

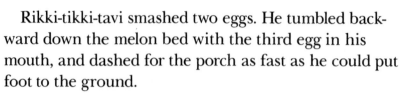

Rikki-tikki-tavi smashed two eggs. He tumbled backward down the melon bed with the third egg in his mouth, and dashed for the porch as fast as he could put foot to the ground.

Teddy and his mother and father were there for an early breakfast, but Rikki-tikki-tavi saw that they were not eating anything. They sat stone still. Their faces were white.

Nagaina was coiled up on the mat by Teddy's chair, within easy striking distance of Teddy's leg. She was swaying to and fro, singing a song of battle.

"Son of the big man who killed my Nag," she hissed. "Stay still. I am not ready yet. Wait a little. Keep very still, all you three. If you move, I strike. And if you do not move, I strike. Oh, foolish people who killed my Nag!"

Teddy's eyes were fixed on his father. All his father could do was whisper, "Sit still, Teddy. You mustn't move. Teddy, stay still."

Then Rikki-tikki-tavi came up and cried, "Turn round, Nagaina. Turn and fight!"

"All in good time," said she, without moving her eyes. "I will settle with *you* soon. But, for now, look at your friends, Rikki-tikki-tavi. They are still and white with fear. They dare not move. And if you come a step nearer, I strike."

"Look at your eggs," said Rikki-tikki-tavi. "In the melon bed near the wall. Go and look, Nagaina."

The big snake turned half round, and saw the egg that Rikki was holding. "Ah-h! Give it to me," she said.

Rikki-tikki put his paws one on each side of the egg. His eyes were blood-red. "What price for a snake's egg? For a young cobra? For a young king cobra? For the last—the very last of the brood? The ants are eating all the others down by the melon bed."

Nagaina spun clear round, forgetting everything for the sake of the one egg. Rikki-tikki-tavi saw Teddy's father shoot out a big hand, catch Teddy by the shoulder, and drag him across the table with the teacups, safe and out of reach of Nagaina.

"Tricked! Tricked! Tricked! *Rikk-tikk,*" chuckled Rikki-tikki-tavi. "The boy is safe. And it was I—I—I that caught Nag last night."

Then he began to jump up and down, all four feet together. "He threw me to and fro, but he could not shake me off! He was dead before the big man blew him in two. I did it. *Rikki-tikki-tavi!* Come then, Nagaina! Come and fight with me."

Nagaina saw that she had lost her chance of killing Teddy, and there was her last egg, between Rikki's paws. In a rage, she gathered herself together and struck out at him.

Rikki-tikki-tavi jumped up and backward.

Again and again she struck. Each time her head lashed out, but she missed. And each time she gathered herself together like a watch-spring to strike again.

Rikki-tikki-tavi danced in a circle to get behind her.

Nagaina spun round to keep her head to his head. The rustle of her tail on the mat sounded like dry leaves blown along by the wind.

In the heat of the battle, Rikki-tikki-tavi had forgotten about the egg. It lay on the floor of the porch, and Nagaina came nearer and nearer to it. At last, while Rikki-tikki-tavi was drawing breath, she caught it in her mouth, turned toward the garden, and flew like an arrow down the path.

Rikki-tikki-tavi knew he must catch her, or all the trouble would start again. She headed straight for the long grass by the bushes. As she plunged into the rathole where she and Nag used to live, Rikki-tikki-tavi's little white teeth closed on her tail, and he went down with her.

Very few mongooses, however wise and old they may be, care to follow a cobra into its hole. It was dark in the hole. Rikki-tikki-tavi never knew when it might open out and give Nagaina room to turn and strike at him, but he held on and stuck out his feet to act as brakes in the dark earth.

In a moment the grass by the mouth of the hole stopped waving. All the birds and frogs and ants in the garden watched and waited. There was no sound, no movement where Nagaina and Rikki-tikki-tavi had disappeared.

Then, all at once, the grass quivered again, and Rikki-tikki-tavi, covered with dirt, dragged himself out of the hole, leg by leg.

"It is all over," he said. "Nagaina will never come out again."

That set all the birds in the garden singing, and the frogs croaking.

When Rikki-tikki-tavi got back to the house, Teddy's mother came out and almost cried over him. That night he ate all that was given him till he could eat no more. Then he went to sleep on Teddy's shoulder, where Teddy's mother saw him when she came to look late at night.

"He saved our lives and Teddy's life," she whispered to her husband. "Just think, he saved all our lives!"

At the sound of her whisper, Rikki-tikki-tavi woke up with a jump, for all mongooses are light sleepers. "Oh, it's you," said he. "That's all right. And you needn't worry. All the cobras are dead, and if they weren't, I'm here."

The little mongoose had a right to be proud of himself, but he did not grow too proud. And he kept that garden as a good mongoose should keep it, with tooth and jump and spring and bite, till never a cobra dared show its head inside the walls.

UNIT FOUR

Nature and Nonsense

The Blue Jay Yarn

by

MARK TWAIN

nimals talk to each other, of course. There can be no question about that. But I suppose there are very few people who can understand them. I never knew but one man who could. I knew he could, however, because he told me so himself.

He was a miner who had lived in a lonely corner of California among the woods and mountains a good many years. He had studied the ways of his only neighbors, the beasts and the birds, until he believed he could understand any remark which they made.

This was Jim Baker. According to Jim Baker, some animals have only a limited education and use only very simple words and scarcely ever a comparison or a flowery figure. But other animals have a large vocabulary and a fine command of language. These latter talk a great deal. They like it. They are conscious of their talent, and they enjoy showing off.

Baker said that blue jays were the best talkers he had found among birds and beasts. Said he:

"There's more to a blue jay than any other creature. He's got more moods and more different kinds of feelings than other creatures. And, mind you, whatever a blue jay feels, he can put into language. And no mere commonplace language, either, but rattling, out-and-out book-talk! Bristling with metaphor, too—just bristling!

175

And as for command of language, why *you* never see a blue jay get stuck for a word. Nobody ever did. They just boil out of him.

"Now, on top of this, there's another thing: a jay can outswear any miner. You think a cat can swear. Well, a cat can. But you give a blue jay a subject that calls for his reserve powers, and where is your cat? Don't talk to me—I know too much about this thing. Now I'm going to tell you a perfectly true fact about some blue jays.

"When I first begun to understand jay language, there was a little incident happened here. Seven years ago the last man in this region but me moved away. There stands his house—been empty ever since—a log house with a plank roof. Just one big room and no more—no ceiling, no floor. Just the plank roof and the log walls. Nothing between that roof and the ground but some weeds growing inside the half-open door.

"Well, one Sunday morning I was sitting out here in front of my cabin, when a blue jay lit on that house, with an acorn in his mouth, and says, 'Hello, I reckon I've struck something.' When he spoke, the acorn dropped out of his mouth and rolled down the roof, of course. But he didn't care. His mind was all on the thing he had struck. It was a knothole in the roof.

"He cocked his head to one side, shut one eye, and put the other one to the hole, like a possum looking down a jug. Then he glanced up with his bright eyes, gave a wink or two with his wings, and says, 'It looks like a hole, it's located like a hole—blamed if I don't believe it *is* a hole!' Then he cocked his head down and

took another look. He glances up perfectly joyful this time, winks his wings and his tail both, and says, 'If I ain't in luck! Why, it's a perfectly elegant hole!'

"So he flew down and got that acorn, and fetched it up and dropped it in. He was just tilting his head back with the happiest smile on his face, when all of a sudden the smile faded off his face and the strangest

look of surprise took its place. Then he says, 'Why, I didn't hear it fall.'

"He cocked his eye at the hole again and took a long look, raised up and shook his head. Then that jay stepped around to the other side of the hole and took another look from that side, and shook his head again.

"He studied a while. Then he went into the details—walked round and round the hole and spied into it from every point of the compass. No use. Now he took a thinking attitude on the comb of the roof, and scratched the back of his head with his right foot a minute, and finally says, 'Well, it's too many for me, that's certain; must be a mighty long hole; however, I ain't got no time to fool around here, I got to 'tend to business; I reckon it's all right—chance it, anyway.'

"So he flew off and fetched another acorn and dropped it in, and tried to flirt his eye to the hole quick enough to see what become of it, but he was too late. He held his eye there as much as a minute; then he raised up and sighed, and says, 'Confound it, I don't seem to understand this thing. However, I'll tackle her again.'

"He fetched another acorn and done his level best to see what become of it, but he couldn't. He says, 'Well, *I* never struck no such a hole as this before; I'm of the opinion it's a totally new kind of a hole.' Then he began to get mad. He held in for a spell, walking up and down the comb of the roof and shaking his head and muttering to himself; but his feelings got the upper hand of him, presently, and he broke loose and cussed himself black in the face. I never see a bird take on so about a little thing. When he got through he walks to the hole and looks in again for a half a minute; then he says, 'Well, you're a long hole, and a deep hole, and a mighty singular hole altogether—but I've started in to fill you and fill you I will, if it takes a hundred years!'

"And with that, away he went. You never see a bird work so since you was born. He laid into his work, and the way he hove acorns into that hole for about two hours and a half was one of the most exciting and astonishing spectacles I ever struck. He never stopped to take a look any more—he just hove 'em in and went for more. Well, at last he could hardly flop his wings, he was so tuckered out. He comes a-drooping down once more, sweating like an ice pitcher, drops his acorn in, and says, 'Now I guess I've got the bulge on you!'

"So he bent down for a look. If you'll believe me, when his head come up again he was just pale with rage. He says, 'I've shoveled acorns enough in there to keep the family thirty years, and if I can see a sign of one of 'em I wish I may land in a museum with a belly full of sawdust in two minutes!'

"He just had strength enough to crawl up on to the comb and lean his back agin the chimbly, and then he collected his impressions and begun to free his mind. I see in a second that what I had mistook for profanity in the mines was only just the rudiments, as you may say.

"Another jay was going by and heard him doing his devotions and stops to inquire what was up. The sufferer told him the whole circumstances, and says, 'Now yonder's the hole, and if you don't believe me, go and

look for yourself.' So this fellow went and looked, and comes back and says, 'How many did you say you put in there?' 'Not any less than two tons,' says the sufferer.

"The other jay went and looked again. He couldn't make it out, so he raised a yell, and three more jays come. They all examined the hole, they all made the sufferer tell it over again, then they all discussed it, and got off as many leather-headed opinions about it as an average crowd of humans could have done.

"They called in more jays; then more and more, till pretty soon this whole region 'peared to have a blue flush about it. There must have been five thousand of them; and such another jawing and disputing and ripping and cussing, you never heard. Every jay in the whole lot put his eye to the hole and delivered a more chuckle-headed opinion about the mystery than the jay that went there before him. They examined the house all over, too. The door was standing half open, and at last one old jay happened to light on it and look in.

"Of course, that knocked the mystery galley-west in a second. There lay the acorns, scattered all over the floor. He flopped his wings and raised a whoop. 'Come here!' he says. 'Come here, everybody; hanged if this fool hasn't been trying to fill up a house with acorns!' They all came a-swooping down like a blue cloud, and, as each fellow lit on the door and took a glance, the whole absurdity of the contract that the first jay had tackled hit him home, and he fell over backward suffocating with laughter, and the next jay took his place and done the same.

"Well, sir, they roosted around here on the housetop and the tree for an hour, and guffawed over that thing like human beings. It ain't any use to tell me a blue jay hasn't got a sense of humor, because I know better. And memory, too. They brought jays here from all over the United States to look down that hole, every summer for three years. Other birds too. And they could all see the point, except an owl that come from Nova Scotia to visit the Yosemite, and he took this thing in on his way back. He said he couldn't see anything funny in it. But then he was a good deal disappointed about Yosemite, too."

The Sunflower

a traditional Japanese poem

A rainy day in June, yet see,—
The sunflower turns its face
Toward the spot where the sun should be.

Apollo and the Sunflower

by

THOMAS BULFINCH

There was once a water nymph named Clytie. She was in love with the sun god, Apollo, but he did not return her love. So she pined away sitting all day long upon the cold ground, with her long hair streaming over her shoulders.

Nine days she sat and tasted no food. Her own tears were her only drink. She gazed steadily on the sun when he rose, so great was her love for the sun god, Apollo. As the sun passed through his daily course to his setting, she looked upon no other object. Her face was always turned toward the sun.

At last, they say, her limbs took root in the ground, and her face became a flower, which turns on its stem so as always to face the sun throughout its daily course. For the sunflower retains, to that extent, the feeling of the nymph Clytie from whom it sprang.

Claude Monet
The Artist's Garden at Vetheuil
National Gallery of Art, Washington, D.C., Ailsa Mellon Bruce Collection

185

The Angler and the Fish

from

AESOP'S FABLES

An angler had been fishing all day and had not caught anything. At the end of the afternoon, however, he did catch one very small fish.

"Please let me go, Master," begged the little fish. "Spare me so that I may grow. If you throw me back into the river now, you can return and catch me again when I am bigger. Then I will make a fine supper, but now I am hardly worth cooking."

The angler shook his head and replied, "No, no, my little fish. I am very hungry, and now that I have caught you, I intend to hold on to you. If I threw you back into the water in hopes of catching you again when you are bigger, I would be very foolish indeed. I would deserve to stay hungry now and hereafter. Small as you are, you will do for my supper tonight."

What you have now is worth more than
what you may (or may not) have later.

How Jahdu Became Himself

from THE TIME-AGO TALES OF JAHDU

by VIRGINIA HAMILTON

Summer had come to the good place called
Harlem. The window was open wide in Mama Luka's
hot little room. Mama Luka had moved her chair closer
to the window. Yes, she had. She had raised her blind so
that she could see what happened in the street below.

"Yes, child," she said to Lee Edward, who sat on the
floor. "I have seen fifty summers come to that street
down there and with each summer will come Jahdu
just running along."

"Will I get to see him this summer?" asked Lee Edward.

"You might have a hard time seeing him, Little Brother,"
Mama Luka said. "Jahdu is never the same."

"Not even his face?" asked Lee Edward. He hoped this

time to catch Mama Luka before she had time to think.

"Anyone who has seen the face of Jahdu will tell you *only* that it is never the same," said Mama Luka carefully. "But there is a steady light from his eyes," she said. "There is pride in his face that is always the same."

"I will look for Jahdu," said Lee Edward. "I will look for the pride in every face I see."

"You know, I start baking bread in the summertime," Mama Luka told Lee Edward. "I always think that maybe this time Jahdu will stop and visit with me and tell me what he has been up to."

"Has Jahdu ever stopped by to visit with you?" asked Lee Edward.

Mama Luka stared out her window. She spoke softly to Lee Edward. "I am baking bread right now," she said. "I am baking bread and I am hoping."

"I can smell the bread," Lee Edward said. "It smells very good, too."

"Yes, child," said Mama Luka, turning from the window. "I never told you before, but Jahdu was born in an oven beside two loaves of baking bread." Mama Luka smiled. "One loaf baked brown and the other baked black. Jahdu didn't bake at all. But since that time black and brown have been Jahdu's favorite colors and the smell of baking bread is the sweetest smell to him."

Then Lee Edward pointed to the windowsill all of a sudden. Mama Luka understood and she cupped her hands around the place Lee Edward had pointed to. Mama Luka opened her mouth and swallowed what had been in her hands.

189

"Oh, yes," she said. "Little Brother, that's the best old story you picked out of the air. It makes me feel cool and fresh inside."

"Then tell it," Lee Edward said to Mama Luka.

"I'm getting myself ready," said Mama Luka.

THIS IS THE JAHDU STORY SO COOL AND FRESH THAT MAMA LUKA TOLD TO LEE EDWARD.

Jahdu was running along. He was telling everybody to get out of his way. Everybody always did get out of Jahdu's way. Except this time somebody wouldn't and that somebody was Grass.

Grass lay on the ground in one dull shade of gray as far as the eye could see. Jahdu shouted at him. "Get out of the way, Grass, for Jahdu is coming through."

Grass didn't move at all. No, he didn't. Jahdu lay down on Grass and stretched himself out as far as he could.

"How do you like that, Uncle No-Color?" Jahdu said to Grass. "Jahdu is heavy, isn't he?"

Grass didn't say a word. But Grass couldn't feel the sunlight with Jahdu stretched out on him and he grew cold. And when Jahdu called him Uncle No-Color, he became very angry.

Grass lifted all his young gray blades straight as arrows. He pushed them against Jahdu with all his might. And the strain on his young gray blades turned each and every one of them green. To this day you can tell Grass whenever you chance to see him. For each and every one of his blades is still green.

Well, Jahdu laughed. He got up slowly. He yawned

two or three times and gave no more thought to Grass, who had turned green.

Jahdu kept right on running along. He was running eastward, for he had been born in the East. And Jahdu had an idea he might like to be born again into something else. He ran and he ran until he came to dry, hot sand.

"Woogily!" Jahdu whispered. "This sand is hotter than anything I know that is hot."

Jahdu saw Ocean lying as calm as could be on the horizon where the hot sand ended.

Jahdu screamed in his meanest voice. "Hey, Uncle Calm Ocean! Why don't you once in a while get up and give the sand something to cool itself with? Lying around all day, watering the clouds and cooling off the birds. Why don't you get yourself together long enough to help out the hot sand?"

Old Ocean wasn't bad. But he was used to being the biggest somebody around under the sky. He was used to not moving, just lying there as cool and blue as he pleased. Ocean knew he was bigger and wetter and deeper than anything under the sun. And when Jahdu said what he had, all grew still. The wind stopped its blowing. Ocean himself stopped being lazy long enough to think about what Jahdu had said.

All at once Ocean gathered himself together right across his middle. He gave a heave that lifted his body higher than he had ever lifted it before. Ocean started moving from the horizon over the sand in a white, foaming line treetop tall.

"Woogily!" said Jahdu. And he went on running.

Old Ocean leaped right in front of Jahdu. But Ocean didn't catch Jahdu. For Jahdu surely knew how to keep running along. Every time Ocean slid back to the horizon to gather himself together again, Jahdu would run away somewhere else. Ocean would hit the hot sand with all his might only to find that Jahdu had run by.

To this day Ocean keeps on moving up and back and up and back again. He keeps on trying to catch anything passing by.

Jahdu kept right on running along. He was growing tired. He felt like stopping to rest. But he had no friend he could stop along with. He had played so many tricks nobody trusted him.

Mrs. Alligator used to give Jahdu free rides on her back. But not anymore, for Jahdu had come along one time with a can of blue paint on his head. He had put Mrs. Alligator to sleep and then he had painted her skin with two coats of blue paint. The paint hadn't worn off for a year. Now Mrs. Alligator thought Jahdu had manners worse than a crocodile's. Whenever she heard Jahdu running along, she would dive deep to the bottom of her pool. Yes, she would.

Jahdu came alongside a shade tree. The shade tree had leaves as big as elephant's ears. It had a trunk smooth to lean against. So Jahdu sat himself down. He leaned against the tree trunk and rested. He let the leaves as big as elephant's ears fan him. Jahdu soon felt like taking a nap. He was almost asleep when he heard a voice next to him.

"Stranger, kindly move off my tail!" said the voice.

"Hey, you, sir, who will lean against a body without a pardon me!"

"Woogily!" said Jahdu, and he jumped five feet away from the tree.

It wasn't the shade tree who had spoken. Shade trees do not speak and do not care who leans against them. It was old Chameleon who had spoken. Chameleon was a lizard six inches long. He had not seen Jahdu for many a month. But when Jahdu said "Woogily!" Chameleon knew him right away.

"Jahdu," Chameleon said, "I wish you would learn to ask somebody when you want to lean on somebody."

Jahdu looked all around. It took him a minute to see the lizard on the tree trunk. Jahdu had always liked Chameleon. Chameleon could change the color of his skin any time he felt like it. If Chameleon sat down on a green leaf, he would turn himself green and nobody could tell he was sitting on the leaf. If he wanted to sit on a flat stone, he would turn himself the color of the flat stone. And nobody need know he was resting awhile.

At last Jahdu saw Chameleon on the trunk of the shade tree. Chameleon was brown as was the dark brown tree trunk.

"Well, how are you doing?" Jahdu said, coming closer.

"You stay right where you are!" shouted Chameleon. "Don't come any nearer until you promise you won't tie my tail in a knot."

"Oh, my goodness," Jahdu said, sitting down.

"I mean what I say," Chameleon told Jahdu. "The last

195

time you tied my tail up I had an awful time getting it untied."

"How *did* you get it untied?" Jahdu wanted to know. He spoke to the lizard in his kindest voice. For Jahdu knew now that he wanted something special from the lizard.

"Never you mind how I got myself loose," said Chameleon. "You just promise."

So Jahdu promised. Then he and the lizard sat against the trunk of the shade tree.

"I've just been running along," Jahdu told his friend Chameleon.

"All right," said Chameleon.

"I had a little fun with Grass," said Jahdu.

"That's good," said the lizard. "Grass is always so gray and sad."

"Not anymore," Jahdu said. "Grass is now green as he can be!"

"All right," Chameleon said. "Green is brighter than gray."

"I had a little fun with Ocean," Jahdu told his friend.

"That's all right," said Chameleon. "Ocean always did lie too far back on the horizon."

"Not anymore," Jahdu told him. "Now Ocean rises tree-top tall. He runs over the hot sand hilltop high and then he falls down trying to catch anything running along."

"That's good, too," said the lizard. "Now the hot sand will get a chance to cool itself."

"So I have stopped awhile from running along," said Jahdu.

"All right," Chameleon said.

"I have stopped and now I know why I was running along and what I want from you," said Jahdu.

"Tell me then," said the lizard.

"I want to know how you work your magic," said Jahdu.

"You already have your own magic," Chameleon told Jahdu. "You can put anything to sleep and wake anything up again."

"But I need to know the magic you have," said Jahdu to his friend.

"What magic is that?" Chameleon asked Jahdu.

"You can change to look like a stone or even a leaf," Jahdu told him.

"Sure I can," said the lizard, "but I can't let you do that, too."

"Well, I know you can't, my friend," Jahdu said. "I only want to know how you do it. If I know how it is you can change and hide, maybe I can learn how to just change into something else."

"Change into what?" Chameleon wanted to know.

"Change myself into whatever I want," Jahdu told him. "If I see a deer, I can be a deer running through the woods. If I see a fox, I can be as swift and clever as a fox."

Chameleon smiled. "It's not hard," he told Jahdu. "I will tell you what I do. With a bit of practice maybe it will work for you."

"Tell me then," said Jahdu.

"First I see a place where I want to sit," Chameleon said. "Then I think about what it feels like sitting there. Next I run as fast as I can to get there. And then I sit. And the color of the thing I'm sitting on comes over me right away."

"That's all you do?" Jahdu asked. "Woogily!" he said. "Changing is going to be easy!"

Suddenly Jahdu looked unhappy. "How am I going to run fast enough to catch up with a deer and climb on his back?" he asked the lizard.

"Maybe you won't have to run at all," said Chameleon. "Maybe you will only need to see the deer running fast."

"Then what?" Jahdu asked.

"Then you think hard," said Chameleon. "You say to yourself, 'Jahdu is running as fast as that deer. Jahdu is on that deer. Jahdu *is* that deer!' "

"Woogily!" said Jahdu.

"Try it," Chameleon told Jahdu.

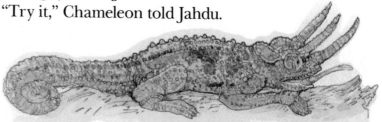

Jahdu left his friend Chameleon dozing against the trunk of the shade tree. Jahdu went running along. He had not seen anything yet that he wanted to be. He was still running eastward to where he had been born.

"The first thing I see that I like, I will be," Jahdu said to himself. And he kept right on running along.

Jahdu came to an island. The island had buildings higher than high. Jahdu liked the buildings. Yes, he did.

He said, "Woogily!" and kept on running. "I'm going to make myself into a building."

Jahdu picked out for himself a building higher than a hilltop. He thought very hard. "Jahdu is running to that building," he said to himself. "Jahdu is on top of that building. Jahdu *is* that building!"

Jahdu became a building made of steel and concrete. He was very tall, but he could not move. Jahdu did not like standing still.

"Woogily!" said Jahdu. He thought very quickly and he said to himself, "Jahdu is jumping off this building. Jahdu is running away from this building. Jahdu is not a building anymore!"

Jahdu kept right on running along. He ran and he ran through the city on an island. He saw a stray cat and he became the cat. But Jahdu didn't like being a cat. He was always hungry. He was sick and he was tired and he slept where he could. Jahdu was thrown out of a supermarket for trying to get at the frozen fish.

"Woogily!" said Jahdu. "Cats have a hard time getting along. Jahdu is jumping off this cat. Jahdu is running faster than this cat. Jahdu is not a cat anymore!"

Jahdu kept on running. He saw an orange-and-black taxicab.

"Woogily!" said Jahdu. "I'm going to be that taxicab." And so he was.

Now Jahdu was busy taking people from one place to another. But he didn't much like being a taxicab. People sat down too hard on his seats and tracked dirt in on his floor. People were afraid when he went very fast. Jahdu worked for long hours. Yes, he did. And the bright lights of the city hurt his eyes.

"Jahdu is jumping off this taxicab," Jahdu said at the end of a long day. "Jahdu is moving faster than that pretty

199

orange-and-black taxicab. Jahdu is not a taxicab anymore!"

The taxicab drove away. Jahdu kept right on running along. He found himself in a fine, good place called Harlem. Yes, he did.

"Woogily!" said Jahdu. "All the people here are brown and black."

Jahdu came upon a group of children playing in a playground. He saw a small, black boy who was running around making noise.

"Woogily!" said Jahdu. "Jahdu is running as fast as that black child. Jahdu is jumping on that black child. Jahdu *is* that black child!"

Black was Jahdu's favorite color and Jahdu was now a strong, black child. He didn't own a baseball or a bat. But he had a dog. Yes, Jahdu did. And the dog's name was Rufus. And the dog was black all over, just like Jahdu. Jahdu had a sister and a brother too. And Jahdu had a good time in the city on the island.

Jahdu was happy. He was a strong, black boy. For a while he stayed in the neighborhood, just enjoying himself.

THIS IS THE END OF THE JAHDU STORY SO COOL AND FRESH THAT MAMA LUKA TOLD TO THE CHILD, LEE EDWARD.

"You picked the story," Mama Luka said. "It was a good story and Jahdu was happy being a strong, black boy."

"The way I am happy?" asked Lee Edward.

"Just the way you are happy," said Mama Luka.

"Did the strong, black boy have the Jahdu magic?" asked Lee Edward.

"The strong, black boy was still a small, black boy," said Mama Luka. "And, Little Brother, a small, black boy doesn't have too much magic, even when he's Jahdu. He could put his mama to sleep by making her read him one storybook after another. And he could wake his papa up fast enough by saying he had been a building once upon a time. But he didn't have much more magic than that."

"I don't see how Jahdu of all the Jahdu stories could like being a small, black child," said Lee Edward. "I would think he'd rather be a building."

"You think about it for a while," Mama Luka told Lee Edward. "I'll take myself a little nap for five or six minutes." Mama Luka always did like sleeping after telling a good Jahdu story.

Mama Luka went right to sleep in her chair and sitting on her long black braid. The smell of baking bread was strong and sweet in the room.

Lee Edward went to Mama Luka's kitchen, not much bigger than a closet, on one side of the room. He peeked into the oven. The large loaf of bread he found had baked brown and was done. Lee Edward took the loaf of bread out of the oven and placed it on the counter.

He turned off the oven and stood sniffing the bread that smelled sweeter than anything. And then Lee Edward lay on his back on the floor beside Mama Luka's chair and thought about Jahdu.

Pretty soon Lee Edward closed his eyes and smiled. A little later he opened his eyes and laughed. He knew why Jahdu was happy being a strong, black boy.

Lee Edward imagined Jahdu's changing from a strong, black boy into a bigger, stronger boy. As Jahdu grew, he had more and more magic power. Something Mama Luka had said about Jahdu came to him.

"There is pride in his face that is always the same."

Little Brother had to smile.

"Once he's grown up he'll be a black Jahdu with all his power," whispered Lee Edward.

He pointed to a space of air close to Mama Luka's right foot. He thought he felt himself growing.

"I can have the pride and the power, too," Lee Edward said, and he waited for Mama Luka to wake up.

I hoped to find some fresh water near the sea, but there was no sign of a river or spring. I walked alone to a part of the shoreline that was bare and rocky. There I climbed a hill from which I could see most of the beach.

And what should meet my eyes but the sight of my shipmates rowing back to the *Adventure* without me! I was about to shout to them when I saw a huge creature walking after them in the sea. The water was barely up to his knees! He was taller than a church steeple!

But the men were almost back to the ship. I could see that they would get away, but I dared not think what this meant for me. Suppose this giant turned back and spotted me.

I ran inland as fast as I could and soon found myself in a field of corn that grew at least forty feet high.

Then I heard a noise, high in the air like thunder, and I saw a huge foot coming toward me. Again that noise—followed by the sound of falling stalks of corn! Then I knew that a giant of a man was cutting the corn and I was soon to be buried under it. I screamed as loud as fear could make me.

The huge farmer stood motionless.

I screamed again. "Stop!"

He bent down and looked about on the ground for some time. At last he spotted me. Then he reached out carefully, as if he were going to touch a small but deadly creature that might bite or sting him.

Finally, the farmer picked me up between his thumb and forefinger and held me about three yards from his eyes.

205

There I hung, more than sixty feet from the ground, pinched most painfully in his grasp.

I groaned loudly. That seemed to let him know how much the pressure of his thumb and finger hurt me. Gently he put me back on the ground on all fours, and knelt to watch me.

At once I got to my feet and made a low bow to him.

He spoke, and his voice was so loud that it made my ears ring.

I shouted words of greeting to him, first in English, then in other languages. But we could not understand each other.

Taking out his handkerchief, he spread it on his open hand which he placed flat on the ground. He motioned for me to step up on it. I did, and he carried me to his house.

There he opened the handkerchief and showed me to his wife. She screamed and ran back as if I had been a bug. But when she took a closer look at me and saw how gentle I was, she was eager to make a pet of me.

At dinner the farmer placed me on the table which was thirty feet high. I kept as far as I could from the edge for fear of falling. His wife gave me some bread crumbs which were as large as loaves to me. I found their scraps of meat too tough to chew.

In the middle of the meal I heard a noise like that of a dozen weavers at work. Turning my head, I discovered it to be the purring of a cat three times the size of an ox. The fierce look of this cat terrified me. But a more fearful danger yet was on the way to the table.

A nurse came in with a baby about a year old in her arms. When the baby spied me, he yelled to have me for a plaything.

The mother, being very foolish, put me toward the baby, within his reach. Suddenly he seized me and put my head into his mouth. But I screamed so loudly that he got frightened and let me drop. I should certainly have broken all my bones in the fall had not the nurse put out her apron to catch me.

The one I grew to like best in the family was the older daughter. She made a bed for me from the cradle in her dollhouse. I called her Glumdalclitch, or little nurse, and she took very good care of me. She was very good with needle and thread and made me seven new shirts.

It was she who taught me the language of this land. I would point to something, and she would tell me the name of it. In a few days I was able to call out for whatever I needed. Soon I was able to talk with her and with the other people of Brobdingnag, for that was the name of this land of giants.

It now began to be known and talked about in the neighborhood that the farmer had found a strange animal in his field. Soon all the neighbors began to visit him so that they could have a look at me. One friend of his suggested that he take me to market and show me to the crowds for a fee.

The farmer and his daughter took me to many cities. And, I must admit, he made a good sum of money from showing me to the people.

One day we came to the royal city, where I was brought before the queen and her court. I bowed before her, and she held out her little finger for me to kiss.

Thanks to Glumdalclitch, I had learned enough of the language to talk to the queen. She was very kind. She bought me from the farmer and asked Glumdalclitch to stay as my nurse and teacher.

One morning my little nurse put me on the window sill to get some air while she washed my clothes. As soon as she left, some wasps as big as turkeys came flying in. Their droning was louder than bagpipes.

As they flew around me, deafening me with their noise, I was fearful that they would sting me to death. So I drew my sword, ready to defend myself. One came at me and I ran him through. Then another, and again I put my sword to good use. When I killed the third wasp, the rest of them flew away.

Another time, when I needed to defend myself, my sword was of no use to me. I was alone in the garden, and a small white spaniel came sniffing up to me. So quickly did the dog take me up in his mouth that there was no time to call for help. Wagging his tail, he ran straight to the gardener and set me gently on the ground. He had been so well trained that he carried me between his teeth without breaking my skin.

The gardener picked me up and asked me if I were all right. I was so frightened and out of breath that for a moment I could not answer. But soon I realized that I was not hurt. From then on, however, I did not go into the garden alone.

After a while I even worked out a way to read the books of Brobdingnag. The book I wished to read would be opened for me and propped up against the wall. Then a tall ladder would be placed in front of it. I would climb to the top of the ladder where I could begin reading the page. As I finished the first few lines, I would descend a step and read on, going in this way to the bottom of the page. The paper was as thick and stiff as cardboard so I could turn the pages for myself.

Even though I was quite happy in Brobdingnag, I could not help wishing sometimes to be in a country where I did not have to live in fear of being stepped on.

◆　◆　◆　◆

Of course, Gulliver finally gets home again. Even after being shipwrecked in Brobdingnag, the land of the giants, and in Lilliput, the land of tiny people, he sets forth again for more adventures.

A Girl Like You

translated from the Chinese
by Isaac Victor Headland
from the book
MEI LI
by
THOMAS HANDFORTH

We keep a dog to watch the house,
A pig is useful, too,
We keep a cat to catch a mouse,
But what can we do
With a girl like you?

211

The Story of Fidgety Philip

by

HEINRICH HOFFMANN

"Let me see if Philip can
Be a little gentleman.
Let me see if he is able
To sit still for once at table."
Thus Papa bade Phil behave,
And Mamma looked very grave.
But fidgety Phil,
He won't sit still.
He wriggles,
And giggles,
And then, I declare,
Swings backwards and forwards,
And tilts up his chair,
Just like any rocking-horse—
"Philip! I am getting cross!"

See the naughty, restless child
Growing still more rude and wild,
Till his chair falls over quite.
Philip screams with all his might,
Catches at the cloth, but then
That makes matters worse again.
Down upon the ground they fall,
Glasses, plates, knives, forks, and all.
How Mamma did fret and frown,
When she saw them tumbling down!
And Papa made such a face!
Philip is in sad disgrace.

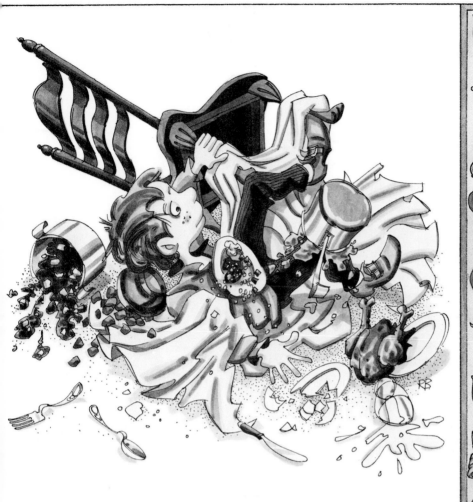

Where is Philip, where is he?
Fairly covered up you see!
Cloth and all are lying on him.
He has pulled down all upon him.
What a terrible to-do!
Dishes, glasses, snapped in two!
Here a knife, and there a fork!
Philip, this is cruel work.
Table all so bare, and ah!
Poor Papa, and poor Mamma
Look quite cross, and wonder how
They shall have their dinner now.

"Run Faster!" Said the Queen

from

THROUGH THE LOOKING-GLASS

by

LEWIS CARROLL

Run faster!" cried the Queen. "Faster, faster!" Then she and Alice ran so fast that they seemed to skim through the air. They hardly touched the ground with their feet. On and on they ran, until Alice was quite out of breath.

Then, all at once, they stopped, and Alice found herself sitting on the ground.

The Queen propped her up against a tree. "You may rest a little now," she said.

Alice looked around her in great surprise. "Why, I do believe we've been under this tree the whole time. Everything's just as it was."

"Of course it is," said the Queen. "What did you expect?"

"Well, in my country," said Alice, "you'd get somewhere else, if you ran very fast for a long time, as we've been doing."

"A slow sort of country," said the Queen. "Now here, you see, it takes all the running you can do to keep in the same place. If you want to get somewhere else, you must run at least twice as fast as that."

Second Fig

by

EDNA ST. VINCENT MILLAY

Safe upon the solid rock the ugly houses stand:
Come and see my shining palace built upon the sand!

A Retrieved Reformation

by

O. HENRY

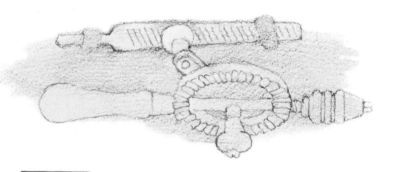

guard came to the prison shoe shop where Jimmy Valentine was working and took him to the front office. There the warden handed Jimmy his pardon, which had been signed that morning.

Jimmy took it in a tired kind of way. He had served nearly ten months of a four-year sentence. He had expected to stay only about three months, at the longest. When a man with as many friends on the outside as Jimmy Valentine had is in jail, it is hardly worth while to cut his hair.

"Now, Valentine," said the warden. "You'll go out in the morning. Brace up. Make a man of yourself. You're not a bad fellow at heart. Stop cracking safes, and live straight."

"Me?" said Jimmy, in surprise. "Why, I never cracked a safe in my life."

"Oh, no," laughed the warden. "Of course not. Let's see, now. How was it you happened to get sent up on that Springfield job? Was it because you wouldn't prove an alibi for fear of hurting someone? Or was it just a case of a mean old jury that had it in for you? It's always one or the other with you innocent ones."

"Me?" said Jimmy. "Why, warden, I never was in Springfield in my life."

"Take him back," said the warden to the guard. "Fix him up with outgoing clothes. Unlock him at seven in the morning. Better think over what I said, Valentine."

At seven the next morning Jimmy stood in the warden's outer office. The warden gave him a railroad ticket and shook hands. Then Mr. James Valentine walked out into the sunshine.

He headed straight for a restaurant. There he tasted the first sweet joys of liberty in the shape of a broiled chicken. From there he went to the train station. He tossed a quarter into the hat of a beggar sitting by the door, and boarded his train.

Three hours set him down in a town near the state line. He went to the café of one Mike Dolan and shook hands with Mike.

"Sorry we couldn't get you out sooner, Jimmy, me boy," said Mike. "But we had that protest from Springfield to buck against. Feeling all right?"

"Fine," said Jimmy. "Got my key?"

He got his key and went upstairs, unlocking the door

of a room at the rear. Everything was just as he had left it. There, on the floor still, was Ben Price's collar button, which had been torn from that detective's shirt when he had arrested Jimmy.

Jimmy slid back a panel in the wall and pulled out a suitcase. He opened it and gazed fondly at the finest set of safecracker's tools in the country. There were drills, braces and bits, and two or three special tools invented by Jimmy himself.

In half an hour Jimmy went downstairs and through the café. He was now dressed in tasteful and well-fitting clothes and carried his suitcase in his hand. He called

for a horse and buggy and waved good-bye to Mike Dolan as he headed back to the train station.

A week after Jimmy Valentine became a free man, there was a neat job of safecracking done in Richmond, Indiana, with no clue to the author. Eight hundred dollars was taken. Two weeks after that, a brand new burglar-proof safe in Logansport was opened like a cheese. That began to interest the detectives. Then an old-fashioned bank-safe in Jefferson City was emptied of all its cash and bank notes. The losses were now high enough to bring the matter up into Ben Price's class of work.

Ben visited the scene of each robbery and was heard to say, "That's Jim Valentine's work. Look at that knob. It was jerked out as easy as pulling up a radish in wet weather. Jimmy never has to drill but one hole. Yes, I guess I want Mr. Valentine—again."

Ben Price knew Jimmy's habits. He had learned them while working on the Springfield case. Long jumps between jobs, quick get-aways, no partners, and a taste for good society—these ways had made Mr. Valentine hard to catch.

One day Jimmy Valentine and his suitcase got off the train at Elmore, Arkansas. Jimmy, looking like a young man just home from college, went down the sidewalk toward the hotel.

A young lady crossed the street, passed him at the corner, and entered a door over which was the sign "The Elmore Bank." Jimmy Valentine looked into her eyes, forgot what he was, and became another man. She

lowered her eyes and colored slightly. Young men of Jimmy's style and looks did not often appear in Elmore.

Jimmy collared a boy who was loafing on the steps of the bank. He began to ask the boy questions about the town, feeding him dimes for each answer. By and by the young lady came out, carefully looked past the young man with the suitcase, and went her way.

"Isn't that young lady Miss Polly Simpson?" asked Jimmy innocently.

"Naw," said the boy. "She's Annabel Adams. Her pa owns this bank. What'd you come to Elmore for? Is that a gold watch chain? I'm going to get a bulldog. Got any more dimes?"

Jimmy went to the Planters' Hotel. He gave his name as Ralph W. Spencer and got a room. He told the desk clerk he had come to Elmore to look for a place to go into business. How was the shoe business, now, in the town? He had thought of starting a shoe business. Was there an opening?

The clerk was happy to tell Jimmy that there ought to be a good opening in the shoe line. There wasn't a store in town that sold just shoes. The dry goods and general store handled them now. Business in all lines was fairly good. Hoped Mr. Spencer would decide to open a shoe store in Elmore. He would find it a pleasant town to live in, and the people very friendly.

Mr. Spencer thought he would stop over in the town a few days and look it over. No, the clerk needn't call the boy. He would carry up his suitcase himself. It was rather heavy.

Mr. Ralph Spencer, the phoenix that arose from Jimmy Valentine's ashes—ashes left by the flame of a sudden love—stayed in Elmore and did well. He opened his shoe store and got a good run of business. He also got to meet Miss Annabel Adams and became even more taken by her charms.

After a year in Elmore, Mr. Ralph Spencer was well thought of by all the people of the town, had a growing business, and was engaged to be married in two weeks

223

to Miss Annabel Adams. Mr. Adams approved of Spencer. Annabel's pride in him almost equalled her love. He was as much at home in the family of Mr. Adams and that of Annabel's married sister as if he were already a member.

One day Jimmy sat down in his room and wrote this letter. He mailed it to the safe address of one of his old friends.

Dear Old Pal,

I want you to be at Sullivan's place in Little Rock next Wednesday night at nine o'clock. I want you to wind up some little matters for me. And, also, I want to make you a present of my kit of tools. I know you'll be glad to get them. You couldn't buy them for a thousand dollars.

Say, Billy, I've quit the old business—a year ago. I've got a nice store. I'm making an honest living. And I'm going to marry the finest girl on earth two weeks from now. It's the only life, Billy—the straight one. I wouldn't touch a dollar of another man's money now for a million.

After I get married, I'm going to sell out and go West where there won't be so much danger of having old scores brought up against me. I tell you, Billy, she's an angel. She believes in me. And I wouldn't do another crooked thing for the whole world. Be sure to be at Sullivan's, for I must see you. I'll bring along the tools with me.

Your old friend,
Jimmy

On Monday night after Jimmy wrote this letter, Ben Price arrived in Elmore. He walked around in his quiet way until he found out what he wanted to know. From the store across the street from Spencer's Shoe Store, he got a good look at Ralph W. Spencer.

"Going to marry the banker's daughter, are you, Jimmy?" said Ben to himself, softly. "Well, I don't know."

The next morning Jimmy had his breakfast at the Adamses' house. He was going to Little Rock that day to order his wedding suit and buy something nice for Annabel. That would be the first time he had left town since he came to Elmore. It had been more than a year since those last "jobs."

After breakfast quite a family party went downtown together—Mr. Adams, Annabel, Jimmy, and Annabel's married sister with her two little girls, aged five and nine. They stopped by the hotel where Jimmy still stayed. He ran up to his room and brought along his suitcase. Then they went on to the bank. There stood Jimmy's horse and buggy and the man who was going to drive him to the train.

All went inside to see Mr. Adams's new safe and vault. Jimmy set his suitcase down. Annabel, whose heart was bubbling with happiness and youth, put on Jimmy's hat and picked up the suitcase. "Wouldn't I make a nice drummer?" said Annabel. "My, Ralph, how heavy your suitcase is! Feels like it was full of gold bricks."

"I have a lot of metal shoehorns in there," said Jimmy, coolly. "I'm going to return them. Thought I'd save mailing charges by taking them back myself."

Mr. Adams was very proud of his new safe and vault. He insisted that everyone should see it. The vault was a

225

small one, but it had a new type of door. It closed with three heavy bolts and a handle, and had a time lock. Mr. Adams beamed as he explained its workings to Mr. Spencer, who showed a polite but not too intelligent interest. The two children, May and Agatha, were delighted by the shining metal and funny clock and knobs.

While they were talking, Ben Price walked in and leaned on his elbow, looking inside. He could see the whole family group, but they could not see him.

Suddenly, there was a scream or two from the women. May, the nine-year-old, in a spirit of play, had shut Agatha in the vault. She had then shot the bolts and turned the knob as she had seen Mr. Adams do.

The old banker sprang to the handle and tugged at it for a moment. "The door can't be opened," he groaned. "The clock hasn't been set yet." Then Agatha's mother screamed again, in panic.

"Hush!" said Mr. Adams, raising his trembling hand. "All be quiet for a moment. Agatha!" he called as loudly as he could. "Listen to me."

During the following silence they could just hear the faint sound of the child wildly screaming in the dark vault.

"My little darling!" wailed the mother. "She will die of fright! Open the door! Oh, break it open! Can't you men do something?"

"There isn't a man nearer than Little Rock who can open that door," said Mr. Adams in a shaky voice. "My God! Spencer, what shall we do? That child—she can't stand it long in there. There isn't enough air—"

Agatha's mother, frantic now, beat the door of the vault with her hands. Annabel turned to Jimmy, her large eyes full of fear, but not yet despairing. To a woman nothing seems quite impossible to the powers of the man she worships.

"Can't you do something, Ralph? Try, won't you?"

He looked at her with a strange, soft smile on his lips. "Annabel," said Jimmy. "Give me that rose you are wearing, will you?"

Hardly believing that she heard him aright, she unpinned the rose from her dress and placed it in his hand.

Jimmy put it into his pocket, threw off his coat, and pulled up his sleeves. With that act, Ralph W. Spencer passed away and Jimmy Valentine took his place.

"Get away from the door, all of you," he said shortly.

He set his suitcase on the table and opened it out flat. From that time on, he seemed unconscious of anyone else. He laid out the shining tools, whistling softly to himself as he always did when at work. In a deep silence, the others watched him as if under a spell.

In a minute Jimmy's pet drill was biting smoothly into the steel door. In ten minutes, breaking his own record, he threw back the bolts and opened the door of the safe.

Agatha was gathered into her mother's arms.

Jimmy Valentine put on his coat and walked toward the front door. As he went, he thought he heard a far-away voice that he once knew call "Ralph!" But he never looked back.

At the door a big man stood somewhat in his way.

"Hello, Ben," said Jimmy, still with his strange smile. "Got around at last, have you? Well, let's go. I don't know that it makes much difference now."

And then Ben Price acted rather strangely.

"Guess you're mistaken, Mr. Spencer," he said. "Don't believe I recognize you. Your buggy's waiting for you, ain't it?"

And Ben Price turned and strolled down the street.

A·C·K·N·O·W·L·E·D·G·M·E·N·T·S

Acknowledgment is gratefully made to the following individuals and publishers for permission to reprint these selections.

"How Ol' Paul Changed the Map of America." From *Yankee Doodle's Cousins* by Anne Malcolmson. © 1941 by Anne Burnett Malcolmson. © renewed 1969 by Anne Malcolmson von Storch. Reprinted by permission of Houghton Mifflin Company.

"True Story." From *Where the Sidewalk Ends* by Shel Silverstein. © 1974 by Evil Eye Music, Inc. Reprinted by permission of Harper & Row, Publishers, Inc.

"Jill Is Given a Task by Aslan." From *The Silver Chair* by C. S. Lewis. Reprinted by permission of Collins Publishers.

"The Scotty Who Knew Too Much." From *Fables for Our Time* by James Thurber. © 1940 by James Thurber. © 1968 by Helen Thurber. Published by Harper & Row, Publishers, Inc.

"The Little Girl and the Wolf." From *Fables for Our Time* by James Thurber. © 1940 by James Thurber. © 1968 by Helen Thurber. Published by Harper & Row, Publishers, Inc.

I·L·L·U·S·T·R·A·T·I·O·N C·R·E·D·I·T·S

Acknowledgment is gratefully made to the following for permission to reprint these illustrations.

PAGE   ILLUSTRATOR

10   Norman Rockwell. "Choosin' Up." Art from the Archives of Brown & Bigelow.

15   Norman Rockwell. Printed by permission of the Estate of Norman Rockwell. © 1916 by the Estate of Norman Rockwell. Photograph courtesy of the *Saturday Evening Post* Marketing Company.

16   Rich Bishop. © 1991 by Jamestown Publishers, Inc. All rights reserved.

22   Robert McCloskey. From *Yankee Doodle's Cousins* by Anne Malcolmson, illustrated by Robert McCloskey. © 1941 by Anne Burnett Malcolmson. © renewed 1969 by Anne Malcolmson von Storch. Reprinted by permission of Houghton Mifflin Company.

25   Rockwell Kent. From *Paul Bunyan* by Esther Shephard, illustrated by Rockwell Kent. © 1924 by Harcourt Brace & World, Inc.

84–105	Sidney Paget. Courtesy of Wilson Library, Special Collections and Rare Books, University of Minnesota, Minneapolis.
107, 109	Tom Feelings. © by Tom Feelings.
111, 116	Courtesy of The Bettmann Archive.
114	Courtesy of Wide World Photos.
118–119	Shonto Begay. © 1991 by Jamestown Publishers, Inc. All rights reserved.
121	Rich Bishop. © 1991 by Jamestown Publishers, Inc. All rights reserved.
122	Burr Shafer. From *Through History with J. Wesley Smith* by Burr Shafer. © 1950 by Burr Shafer. Reprinted by permission of Vanguard Press, a division of Random House, Inc.
123	Winslow Homer. Photograph courtesy of the North Carolina Museum of Art. Painting purchased with funds from the State of North Carolina.
124	Arthur Rackham.
127, 129, 131–134	Ted Harrison. © 1991 by Jamestown Publishers, Inc. All rights reserved.
137	Jan Naimo Jones. © 1991 by Jamestown Publishers, Inc. All rights reserved.
138	Howard Pyle. Photograph courtesy of the Howard Pyle Collection, Delaware Art Museum, Wilmington.

203   Pamela R. Levy. © 1991 by Jamestown Publishers, Inc.

204, 208   Arthur Rackham. The Central Children's Room, Donnell Library Center, The New York Public Library.

211   Thomas Handforth. From *Mei Li* by Thomas Handforth. © 1938 by Thomas Handforth. Reprinted by permission of Doubleday, a division of Bantam, Doubleday, Dell Publishing Group, Inc.

213   Rich Bishop. © 1991 by Jamestown Publishers, Inc.

215   Sir John Tenniel.

216–217   Shonto Begay. © 1991 by Jamestown Publishers, Inc.

218–229   Jan Naimo Jones. © 1991 by Jamestown Publishers, Inc.